Portrait of a Decade

The 1960s

TREVOR FISHER

B.T. Batsford Ltd, London

Contents

The original idea for the Portrait of a Decade series was conceived by Trevor Fisher.

First published 1988
Reprinted 1990

Typeset by Tek-Art Ltd Kent
and printed and bound
in Great Britain by
Courier International Ltd
Tiptree, Essex
for the publishers
B.T. Batsford Ltd
4 Fitzhardinge Street
London W1H 0AH

ISBN 0 7134 5603 5

The frontispiece shows American Civil Rights leader Martin Luther King addressing the march to Washington in 1963.

Introduction

The 1960s have gone down in history as the 'Swinging Sixties' – best remembered for the hippies and the Beatles, the Rolling Stones and the Summer of Love, drugs, flamboyant fashion and the 'permissive society'. But these were just one aspect of a decade which saw enormous change. This book highlights some of the most interesting and important developments, putting them in their wider context and showing their effect on the lives of ordinary people.

Dead Vietcong bodies lie unheeded in a street near Saigon. It was pictures such as this that gave energy to the peace movement; (below) the famous peace poster by John Lennon and Yoko Ono.

A world in conflict

At the end of the 1950s, world politics were still dominated by the conflict between the capitalist nations, led by the USA, and the Communist countries, led by the USSR. However, the bonds which had kept people in both blocs loyal to their leaders were breaking down. In the Communist world, a major split occurred in 1960 between Russia and China. The Chinese decided that the Russians were betraying communism and set off on what they called the 'Cultural Revolution', and, they hoped, world revolution against capitalism.

Within the capitalist world, which experienced a period of relative material prosperity during the 1960s, many people came to distrust their governments and rebel against them. This had already started at the end of the 1950s with the campaign against nuclear weapons, particularly active in Britain, and the black Civil Rights Movement in America. 'Ban the Bomb' was a slogan which could bring thousands of people on to the streets to protest against the threat of nuclear destruction. In the United States even more protested against racial discrimination and the violence used against peaceful civil rights protestors, some of whom were murdered.

The protestors' belief in peaceful demonstration was shaken by their failure to achieve their goals and by the escalating violence in Vietnam. The American government regarded the Vietnam war as part of the struggle between communism and capitalism, which saw conflicts over spying, the Berlin Wall, and Cuba in the first years of the decade. To help stop South-East Asia falling under Communist control the United States began sending military 'advisers' (i.e. troops) to Vietnam in 1960. The violence used by the immensely powerful American forces against a small, backward peasant country in what was the first televised war caused outrage, however. Student 'New Leftists' saw Vietnam as a capitalist obscenity. Moreover, it became clear that despite massive destruction the United States could not win the war, and the world watched amazed as a small peasant army beat the forces of the most powerful country in the world.

During the 1950s the American politician Dean Rusk had said, 'Britain has lost an empire and not found a role'. In the 1960s, Britain still struggled to re-establish her position in the world. She started the decade under the premiership of Harold Macmillan ('Supermac'), but his government floundered amid scandal and economic crisis, and from 1964 to 1970 Labour, under Harold Wilson, ran the country, but without solving its economic problems. Both Macmillan's Tories and Wilson's socialists tried to enter the European Common Market but were blocked by French President, Charles de Gaulle.

Introduction

Peace and love

Julie Christie with the long-haired 'cool' look that set a fashion for girls of the late 1960s.

As a reaction to the growing violence of the 1960s, many people turned to the ideals of peace and love. Ironically, many of those who were seen to be in favour of peace – including President John Kennedy, his brother Bobby, the black civil rights leader Martin Luther King, and many unarmed civil rights workers – were themselves murdered. The horrors of the war in Vietnam dramatized what many saw as a drift towards destruction, and their reaction was to seek a genuinely peaceful way of life. Across the world, youth took up the slogan 'Make Love, not War', and the Love Generation emerged. Many of these were hippies – people who dropped out of conventional society to take up a lifestyle based on peace, loving relationships and often mystical religions. Many more who were not fully hippies were influenced by their ideas and fashions, especially using the soft drug cannabis and the hallucinogenic drug LSD.

Among the latter were the Beatles, who led an astonishing transformation in popular music. At the start of the 1960s pop singers were still seen primarily as performers of other people's songs, and not given much credit as creative artists. By the end of the decade leading pop stars like the singer/songwriter Bob Dylan, and Rolling Stones Mick Jagger and Keith Richard, had established themselves as singers, writers, musicians and charismatic live performers – 'charismatic' being one of the in-words of the 1960s. This was the decade when the children of the post-war baby boom came of age, and their energy poured into politics and the arts.

Sport and the arts

At the start of the 1960s, the cultural world was still largely divided into 'High Art' and 'Popular Art', with a good deal of snobbery attached to the 'High Arts' like theatre, painting, poetry and classical music. 'Pop Art', like film and rock music, was regarded as little more than entertainment and the serious critics ignored it. During the 1960s the division between the two became blurred. Popular films and music received serious attention from the critics, and in Britain even *The Times* carried reviews of pop music. Painters, too, became interested in popular subjects and ideas. There even developed a school of painters called the 'Pop Artists', one of whom, Peter Blake, crossed the divide completely by designing the famous cover for the Beatles album 'Sergeant Pepper' in 1967.

The Beatles appeared on the cover of Sergeant Pepper in the fashion of the year – old military uniforms and droopy moustaches.

This was the decade when national boundaries in art broke down as never before. Pop music again led the way, with pop musicians travelling farther and farther afield, and radio stations all over the world broadcasting white western pop music. The influence wasn't all one way, though. The Beatles, the first British pop group to succeed in America, became greatly influenced by the music of India, and a whole generation of white pop musicians opened their ears to American black soul and blues music. For the first time, black artists found themselves treated as equals. In sport, too, black athletes made more and more impact, with figures such as tennis player Arthur Ashe and boxer Cassius Clay (Muhammad Ali) winning major championships. The exclusion of black stars from South African teams became a major political issue, revealing that racism was still rife in sport. In sport, as in politics and social life, though some blacks made progress toward real equality, on the whole most black people suffered from as much discrimination at the end of the decade as they had done at the start.

The science explosion

Science and technology continued to stride forward in the 1960s at an ever-increasing pace. Advances in transport and telecommunications made the world a smaller place, and sociologist Marshall McLuhan talked of the world as a 'global village'. People could, via television and satellites, plug instantly into news, sport and culture from thousands of miles away. The launch of satellites like Telstar and Early Bird, plus immensely powerful computers, made this possible. Meanwhile, long-distance travel became available for millions of ordinary people with the increasing use of jet aircraft. By the end of the decade there was so much air traffic that the jumbo jet was developed to cope with it.

The growth of high-technology science and engineering scored its most spectacular successes in the space race. In 1960 no human being had ever gone into space. By the end of the decade, people had flown to the moon and close-up pictures of the planets had been taken by probes flying deep in space.

The youth decade

The 1960s, then, did more than just 'swing'. Many of the values and conventions of the immediate post-war world were called into question, and although many of the questions had still not been satisfactorily answered by the end of the decade society would never be the same again. The world had become a smaller and better-informed place. Commentators spoke of an 'information explosion'. Whether or not, however, the development of the 'global village' made the earth a better place in which to live is the main question posed by the events of the seventh decade of the twentieth century.

1960 Spy plane

Hopes for progress dashed

THE SITUATION IN THE COLD WAR between the capitalist countries, led by America, and the Communist countries, led by the Soviet Union, seemed to be improving at the start of 1960. Leaders of the four major world powers – the USA, Britain, France and the USSR – were to meet at a conference in Paris in May. The Russian leader, Nikita Kruschev, described himself as 'optimistic' that progress could be made on world problems.

Then, just before the conference, Kruschev startled the world with a sensational revelation – the Russians had shot down an American spy plane over Russia. On 5 May, Kruschev told the Supreme Soviet (a top government committee) that an American plane had been destroyed in an illegal flight over Soviet territory – and that this was not the first time the Americans had flown over Russia without permission:

A United States aircraft intruded into the airspace of our country on April 9th. . . . The Americans . . . decided to repeat the aggressive act. The date chosen was May 1st. . . . At 5.56 a.m. (Moscow time) an aircraft flew over the frontier and continued into the interior. Orders were given that the aircraft must be shot down . . . the aircraft bore no identification marks but it has been established that it was American. . . .

Accident or trespass?

IT WAS AN ACT OF TRESPASS to fly over another country without permission, and the incident provoked serious consequences. The Americans at first claimed that the plane had entered the Soviet Union by accident, and on 7 May said: 'There has been no deliberate attempt to violate Soviet air space', but as it was clear the plane had been shot down over 1000 miles inside the Soviet Union, the Americans were forced to admit it had been there intentionally. President Eisenhower agreed the flight had been a spying mission, but defended it as a reasonable attempt to get information. He denied it had been aggressive, saying it was not an attack on Russia.

The President . . . challenged Russian pretentions that the United States in some way is on trial for having publicly admitted that the U2 was on a reconnaissance mission – the only way in the modern world, he said, by which they could secure information about a closed society that was constantly threatening to use its strength. 'If they want to say they are putting me on trial, that is their privilege', he remarked, 'but to say that the United States was being tried was another piece of propaganda that distorted facts'.

From *The Times*, 18 August 1960

The wreckage of Gary Powers' plane. Powers parachuted out and landed safely.

The course of the U2 mission, as published by The Times. *The plane was intended to fly on to a US base in Norway.*

crisis

Apology and criticism

WHEN KRUSCHEV ARRIVED IN PARIS on 16 May for the summit conference he called on Eisenhower to apologize for the incident:

The United States government . . . must first condemn the provocative action of the United States air force with regard to the Soviet Union and secondly refrain from continuing these actions.

Eisenhower had already ordered that there should be no more flights, but he was not prepared to criticize his own air force. Many people believed that the American President had himself given permission for the flight. Kruschev was furious that Eisenhower would not apologize and stormed out of the summit conference.

Gary Powers in the dock at his trial in Moscow for spying.

Trial and conviction

IN AUGUST the pilot of the U2 spy plane, Gary Powers, was put on trial in Moscow. On 18 August, he pleaded guilty to spying. He said that he had flown from Adana in Turkey to Peshawar in Pakistan and then across Russia aiming for Norway. He had been told that if he flew at 68,000 ft (21,000 m) he could not be shot down. After his plane crashed, a poison pen, a silent pistol, and pictures of Russian airfields were found inside it.

President Eisenhower, unlike many of his countrymen, today found no evidence of

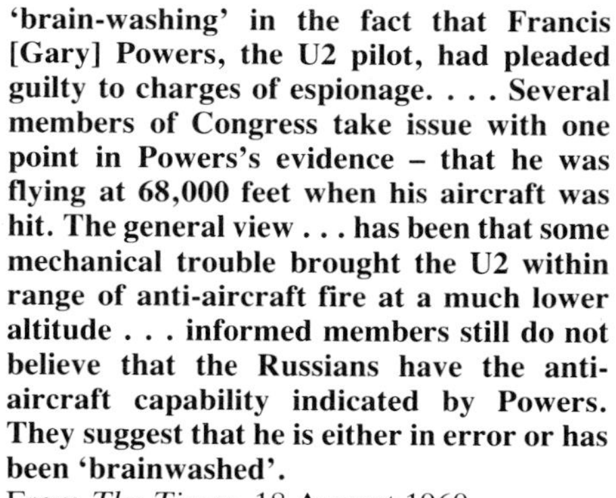

'brain-washing' in the fact that Francis [Gary] Powers, the U2 pilot, had pleaded guilty to charges of espionage. . . . Several members of Congress take issue with one point in Powers's evidence – that he was flying at 68,000 feet when his aircraft was hit. The general view . . . has been that some mechanical trouble brought the U2 within range of anti-aircraft fire at a much lower altitude . . . informed members still do not believe that the Russians have the anti-aircraft capability indicated by Powers. They suggest that he is either in error or has been 'brainwashed'.

From *The Times*, 18 August 1960

Powers was sentenced to ten years in prison. (He was swopped in 1962 for a Soviet spy caught by the Americans.)

Trust torpedoed

THE U2 INCIDENT ended any hopes of friendship between the capitalist and Communist countries. Suspicion and friction developed, and the Chinese Communists told the Russians that Kruschev's hopes for 'peaceful co-existence' between Communists and capitalists were unrealistic as the Americans could not be trusted. Kruschev did not agree, but the Russians did now believe that co-operation between the East and West was no longer possible.

Winds of change in Africa

AT THE BEGINNING OF THE YEAR, the British prime minister, Harold MacMillan, visited Africa. He arrived in South Africa, where the white minority held all the power, and on 3 February told the South African Parliament what he had seen on his tour.

The most striking of all the impressions I have formed since I left London a month ago is the strength of African national consciousness. It is happening everywhere. The wind of change is blowing through the continent.

Macmillan meant by this that the days when white Europeans could run Africa were numbered. The black majority wanted to take over. Events in the Congo were soon to prove him right, but would also show the problems this transfer of power could create.

Congo crisis

BLACK RULE IN AFRICA was not easy to achieve, however. In May, the Belgians decided to leave the Congo, which they had ruled since 1908. In July, the new government faced a crisis when the province of Katanga, under its leader, Tshombe, decided to leave the Congo and form its own separate country. The new black prime minister of the Congo, Lumumba, asked for help from the United Nations. The UN agreed and sent an army. Arguments then broke out between Lumumba and other Congolese politicians, and in September a new prime minister, Ileo, was appointed. Lumumba refused to give way, and for a time there were two prime ministers. The government seemed likely to collapse, and on 15 September the head of the army, General Mobutu, seized power in a military coup.

Massacre at Sharpeville

THE WHITE SOUTH AFRICANS, however, refused to give any power to blacks. Attempts by the Africans to change things were met with violence. On 22 March, a peaceful march in Sharpeville by the Pan Africanist Movement was attacked by armed police. Fifty-six black Africans were shot dead on the spot, including a child, and 162 were wounded. The police argued they were being attacked, but though stones had been thrown in the morning – and there had been one fatal shooting – the Sharpeville march had been non-violent. Indeed, at the inquest on 4 May the Johannesburg district surgeon reported that of 52 dead bodies he examined, two-thirds had been shot in the back. The South African government, however, took no action against the police for the massacre, and on 23 April, Bishop Reeves of Johannesburg, an opponent of the government, left the country fearing imprisonment. On 6 October white South Africa voted to leave the Commonwealth.

The Sharpeville Massacre: an African points to the body of a murdered woman.

Cuban oil and sugar crisis

IN CUBA arguments between the new government of Fidel Castro and the Americans became more bitter. Castro accused the Americans of interfering in Cuba's affairs; America accused Castro of going Communist. Castro had confiscated some American property, but on 24 February offered to discuss this with the Americans. However, this did not stop the Cubans taking over the Texas Oil Company works on 30 June, when the Company refused to handle Russian oil. On 1 July other American oil works were taken over by the Cubans. The Americans then stopped importing Cuban sugar. Sugar was Cuba's main export, and 740,000 tons were due to be sent to the United States that autumn. On 11 July the Soviet Union agreed to take all Cuba's sugar for the next five years. This meant Cuba was able to ignore the American Government – but now relied on Russia. On 8 August £267 million of American property was taken over by the Cuban government, and on 19 September the American banks were nationalized, but the naval base at Guantanamo stayed in American hands. On 30 September the American Government advised all its citizens to leave Cuba, and in October the United States ceased all trading with Cuba.

World News 1960

America's new president

THE UNITED STATES elected a new president in 1960. Eisenhower, the Republican, was stepping down after eight years, and both the Democrat and Republican Parties chose new candidates. The Democrats frontrunner was a 43-year-old Senator, John F. Kennedy. Young and energetic, Kennedy was a Catholic. Most Americans were Protestants. They had never had a Catholic President. Would they vote for one now? On 12 May Kennedy won the support of Democrats in the largely Protestant state of West Virginia, and it seemed that religion would not come into it. On 14 July Kennedy was selected as the Democratic candidate, and on the 30 July the Republicans chose Richard Nixon. Television was now becoming a very important medium, and in September and October the two men held a series of televised debates. Nixon had a problem. Under the bright lights, it looked as though he had not shaved. In the first broadcast he wore heavy make-up, which looked terrible. Many Americans thought he looked dirty. Nixon lost the election by a small majority, and some say the television debates were the reason.

Vietnam

IN 1954 VIETNAM had been divided into the Communist North, under Ho Chi Minh, and capitalist South, under Ngo Dinh Diem, after the Communists had forced the French to abandon Vietnam. Since 1954 a guerrilla force, the National Liberation Front (known as the Vietcong), backed by the North, had been gradually gaining strength. The United States had been sending arms to Diem since 1954, and in 1960 President Kennedy decided to send American military advisors to South Vietnam to train Diem's army.

Supermac

IN BRITAIN THE TORY PARTY was still enjoying its 1959 election success. The reputation of Prime Minister Harold Macmillan ('Supermac') was high, and the Tory Party was united and confident. The last of the wartime controls on British life was lifted with the abolition of conscription – two years' compulsory service in the forces, known as 'National Service' – and a quiet debate on whether Britain should join the Common Market was taking place.

'Ban the Bomb'

THE LABOUR PARTY, by contrast, was racked with bitter arguments and divisions. The main debate was whether or not Britain should follow the policy of the Campaign for Nuclear Disarmament and abandon nuclear weapons. The 'Ban the Bomb' campaign launched in early 1960 was very successful among Labour supporters, many of whom took part in the Easter march from Aldermaston, but Hugh Gaitskell, the Labour leader, and most of the Labour MPs wanted Britain to keep the bomb. On 6 October, at the Labour conference, Frank Cousins, leader of the Transport and General Workers' Union, the biggest trade union, moved a motion calling for 'The complete rejection of any defence policy based on the threat or the use of strategical or nuclear weapons', and it was passed by 43,000 votes. Hugh Gaitskell refused to accept the decision, saying he would 'Fight, fight, and fight again to save the Party we love'. The Labour Party was completely split.

However, some of the CND's supporters were getting tired of waiting. Although the Easter march had attracted 100,000 people, it had had little effect on the government. A group called the Committee of 100 was set up to take non-violent direct action, breaking the law if necessary, to pressurize the government to give up the bomb.

The Aldermaston anti-nuclear march, Easter 1960.

1960 Sport and the Arts

Elvis Presley greets his fans dressed in the uniform of a US soldier.

Films

1960 WAS A GOOD YEAR FOR FILMS. In July, French director Alan Renais' film about the effect of the atom bomb *Hiroshima Mon Amour* ('Hiroshima, My Love') arrived in London, and in February Fellini's film *La Dolce Vita* ('The Sweet Life') opened in Italy. Many people thought it was the first film to show properly the decadence of the affluent society. In May the 'Kitchen Sink' school of realist novels came to the screen with *Saturday Night and Sunday Morning*, directed by Karel Reisz and starring Albert Finney, from the book of the same name. Hollywood also scored successes, including Alfred Hitchcock's terrifying drama of a madman, *Psycho*.

Jazz gets a bad name

MANY YOUNG PEOPLE were already experimenting, trying out alternatives to pop music in folk, blues and jazz. Unfortunately, violence at the Beaulieu jazz festival forced it to close, but others followed.

On the Saturday evening the Johnny Dankworth band was billed to play. . . . During the Dankworth set, the crowd climbed . . . up the scaffolding supporting the TV arc lights (the festival was being televised live), bottles were thrown and the lights temporarily went out. As they came on again a crowd invaded the stage, just as the Bilk band arrived. . . . Acker Bilk went into retreat, his banjoist's instrument smashed. At that point twenty ambulances and five fire engines, alerted by the chaos being broadcast to the nation, arrived on the scene. Gerald Lascelles, cousin to the Queen, ordered a man from the roof. "No", said the man, "not until you say 'please'." "Come down", Lascelles ordered again. "Say 'Please' " said the man. "Oh, all right, 'please' ", said Lascelles. The man came down.

Quoted in Lord Montagu of Beaulieu, *Gilt and Gingerbread*, Michael Joseph, 1967

Books

AN ATMOSPHERE OF FREEDOM and experiment was in the air. In the autumn the novel *Lady Chatterley's Lover* came into the courts. D.H. Lawrence's controversial story about a titled lady who takes a gamekeeper as her lover had long been banned. Penguin books published the unexpurgated text, and the court ruled that since it was a work of art it could not be obscene.

Meanwhile, the TUC passed a resolution, No. 42 on the agenda, calling for the unions to promote the arts. Playwright Arnold Wesker took this as the opportunity to press for a new type of arts festival, Centre 42.

New plays of the year

February:	*Fings Ain't What They Used To Be* by Frank Norman and Lionel Bart
April:	*The Caretaker* by Harold Pinter.
	Rhinoceros by Eugene Ionesco, produced by Orson Welles, starring Laurence Olivier.
	I'm Talking About Jerusalem by Arnold Wesker.
June:	*A Man For All Seasons* by Robert Bolt.
July:	*The Entertainer* by John Osborne, starring Laurence Olivier.

Sporting achievements

IN SPORT, the greatest international event was the Rome Olympics. Two events stood out – Herb Elliott's victory in the 1500 metres, and Cassius Clay's success in the light heavyweight boxing. Elliott, one of the greatest runners of all time, had not been beaten in the 1500 metres or the mile since he was 16. He came into the Rome Olympics as the world record holder at 1500 metres, and scored a double success by taking the gold and cutting 0.4 seconds off his own world record. Less noticeable at the time was the victory of Cassius Clay. Clay's gold medal was the start of an astonishing career.

On the road

In Britain, the motor car continued to be the most popular way of getting from one place to another. Following the opening of the first motorway in Britain, the M1, in 1959, the first motorway café was opened in August. The award-winning mini car from Austin motors had a mini-van version from June. Lionel Bart mentioned the growing traffic jams in his hit song 'Fings Ain't What They Used To Be'.

A report in March warned of the danger to the British car industry from the Japanese. In 1950 the Japanese had made only 20,000 cars, but by 1959 they were making 262,814, and production was growing rapidly. On 3 October a director of the Birmingham Small Arms Company warned of the 'menace' of Japanese competition in world trade.

Fings Aint What They used To Be
They've changed our local Palais
Into a bowling alley an
Fings ain't what they used
to be . . .

There used to be trams,
Not very quick,
Got you from place to place
But now there's just jams,
Half a mile thick
Stopping the human race,
I'm walking . . .

Messages from space

Steady progress was made in space exploration. On 11 March the Americans launched a rocket, Pioneer V, aimed at Venus. This was supposed to send messages back 186 million miles, and though it failed it taught scientists a great deal. On 15 May the Russians launched a 4½-ton spaceship, and announced this was 'another step towards manned space flight'. The ship was big enough to carry a person. The American space programme also scored successes. On 26 May it launched the Midas Experimental satellite, to detect rocket launches in Russia and give America half an hour's warning of attack, and the Samos reconaissance satellite, which was to take pictures of the earth from outer space. The most important satellite, however, was sent up on 13 August. This was Echo 1, little more than a balloon 100 feet (33 metres) in diameter. From its orbit 1000 miles up, it was well placed to bounce radio messages from one point on earth to another. Radio messages were beamed up and back successfully, showing that satellite telecommunications were possible.

Animals in space

The United States and the Soviet Union both sent animals into space to see if living things could survive space travel. The Soviets had put a dog, Laika, into space with their second satellite, but the satellite had crashed and the dog had been killed. On 20 August the Soviets sent up the Korbal satellite with two dogs and other animals and brought it back safely. The animals survived 17 orbits without ill effects. On 13 October the Americans sent up three mice 700 miles and brought them back alive. This was the farthest into space any living things had ever been and survived.

Laika, the first dog in space.

1961 Berlin split

Growing tensions in Berlin

FOLLOWING THE SPY PLANE SCANDAL in 1960, tension between the United States and the Soviet Union remained high in 1961. The most serious incident took place in Germany, where the country was divided into Communist and capitalist areas. Deep inside the Communist part, the German Democratic Republic, was the old capital, Berlin. The four wartime allies, Russia, America, France and Britain, had divided the city between them. The Americans, British and French kept troops in West Berlin, the capitalist part, and insisted the city was still controlled by the four allies. The Russians wanted to hand over the city to the GDR, but the Western allies refused to allow this.

At the start of 1961, Berlin was still run as one city, and people could move freely between East and West Berlin. Many East Berliners lived in the East but worked in the West during the day. This worried the Russians and the East Germans. They feared the growing strength of the West German army, remembering Germany had attacked Russia in 1941. They believed that West Berlin was being used as a base to send spies into East Germany. But, most of all, they disliked the fact that since the end of the war some two million East Germans had gone to live in richer, capitalist West Germany, and most had travelled through Berlin. The East German authorities wanted to stop this.

In February and March, Kruschev argued with the West over how Berlin should be run. He suggested it should become an 'Open City' – i.e., that no troops should be kept there by any country. The West refused this, fearing that East German and Russian troops would move back if they removed their soldiers. Meanwhile, on 18 March, the East Germans admitted there were serious shortages of goods, and announced plans to deal with the problems. Many East Germans were not convinced. Over the Easter holiday 3000 East Germans left East Berlin to become refugees.

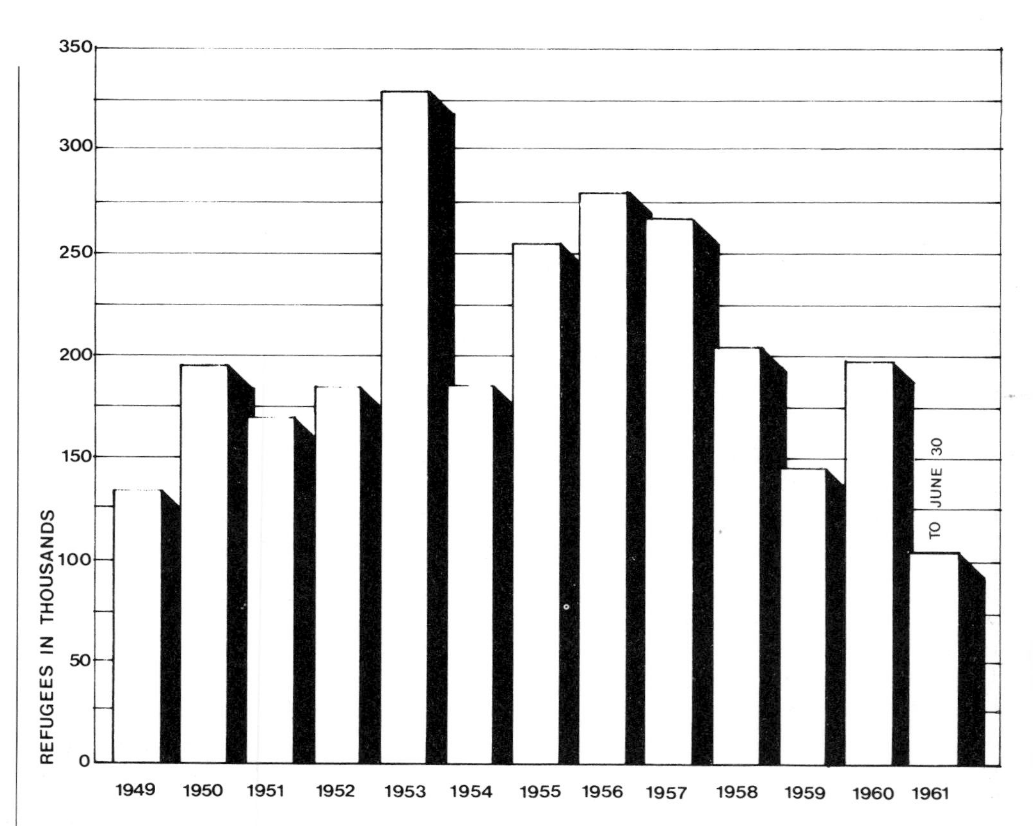

Graph showing the exodus of Germans from East to West Germany between 1949 and 1961. (Source: West German Ministry of Refugees)

Refugees go West

ON JUNE 13 RUSSIA threatened to make a separate treaty with the East Germans, handing over control of East Berlin and the roads to Berlin to the GDR. The Western powers argued that Russia could not break the agreement that Berlin should be run by the four former allies. Meanwhile, the number of refugees was increasing. By July, the average was 870 per day and a total of 30,444 crossed over that month. Most were young: 53.5% were under 25. The East Germans decided they could not afford to lose so many young people. A further 15,000 East Germans fled to West Berlin in August, but by then steps were being taken to seal off the frontier.

by Cold War

A divided city

JUST AFTER 2 a.m. ON 13 AUGUST, trucks containing guards roared around East Berlin, dropping off troops. The soldiers set up barbed-wire fences and machine guns, effectively dividing the city into two. That morning, East Berliners found they could not travel to work in West Berlin – they were turned back. A few crossing points remained, but East Germans were not allowed through. On 17 August the barbed-wire was replaced by a eight-foot [2.5 m] high wall, with watch towers controlled at regular intervals by armed police. In the first year of operation, 41 people were killed trying to cross the wall from East to West. The flow of refugees became a trickle. Communist East Germany had been cut off from the capitalist West.

Reasons for closing the frontier

IN JULY the British *Guardian* newspaper published the following report from Terence Prittie, its Bonn correspondent:

Refugees arriving in West Berlin say that their principal reason for leaving their homes was the fear that the Western garrisons would leave Berlin . . . other contributory factors in this exodus from East Germany are the worsening food situation, the discontent of the dispossessed farmers . . . [and] the passing of a new and repressive labour law. . . . The concern of the East German regime is heightened by the fact that so many young people are seeking refuge in West Germany. This month over half of the East German refugees have been under thirty years of age. . . . Nearly 700 doctors fled to the West in 1960 and there is now often only one doctor left to four or five thousand patients. The East German teaching profession last year [1960] lost 142 university and college lecturers and professors and over 2,000 school teachers.

The official East German reason why the border had to be closed was rather different, as this communiqué of 13 August 1961 from the member-states of the Warsaw Pact shows:

Nowhere else in the world are so many espionage and sabotage centres of foreign states to be found as in West Berlin. . . . These numerous, subversive centres smuggle their agents into the GDR for all kinds of subversion, recruiting spies, and inciting hostile elements to organise sabotage and provoke disturbances in the GDR . . . and for undermining the GDR's economy. Governmental and military agencies of the GFR, [West Germany] through deceit, bribery and blackmail, make some unstable elements in the GDR leave for Western Germany. These deceived people are compelled to serve in the Bundeswehr [West German army] or are recruited to the intelligence services of different countries, to be sent back to the GDR as spies and saboteurs. . .

In the face of the aggressive reactionary aspirations of the reactionary forces of the GFR and its NATO allies, the Warsaw Treaty member-states must take the necessary measures for ensuring their security, and primarily the security of the GDR. . . . The governments of the Warsaw Treaty member-states address to the People's Chamber and Government of the GDR a proposal to establish such control on the borders of West Berlin as would securely block the way to subversive activities against the socialist countries. . .

East German soldiers oversee proceedings as the division between East and West Berlin is made more permanent.

John Kennedy's presidential speech

IN THE UNITED STATES, John Kennedy was sworn in as the youngest-ever President in the country's history. To many people he seemed to offer an optimistic future.

Let the word go forth from this time and place, to friend and foe alike, that the torch has been passed to a new generation of Americans, born in this century, tempered by war, disciplined by a cold and bitter peace . . . and unwilling to witness or permit the slow undoing of those human rights to which this nation has always been committed. . .

Let every nation know, whether it wish us well or ill, that we shall pay any price, bear any burden, meet any hardship, support any friend, oppose any foe, in order to assure the survival and success of liberty. This much we pledge.

Extract from John Kennedy's inaugural speech, January 1961

Civil rights in America

BLACK AMERICANS took the President at his word and pressed for civil rights against racial discrimination. On 20 May, 400 federal marshals (government policemen) had to be sent to Montgomery, Alabama, after a peaceful demonstration by black people had been attacked by a mob of 1500 whites. Local police had refused to act, even though this was the third attack on blacks in a week. On 21 May, 1000 whites attacked the church where the black leader, Martin Luther King, was preaching. The demonstrations continued despite this when black Freedom Riders, calling for civil rights for blacks, marched through Alabama and Mississippi to New Orleans. 27 Black Freedom Riders were arrested when they arrived in Jackson, Mississippi.

Communists disagree over Stalin

RUSSIA, UNDER KRUSCHEV, continued to abandon the ideas of the dead Communist dictator, Stalin, whose word had been law until Kruschev had denounced him in 1956. On 30 October Stalin's body was moved out of the tomb it had shared with the founder of the USSR, Lenin. The small Communist state of Albania disliked Russia's criticisms of Stalin, and on 19 October broke off diplomatic relations. More seriously, Zhou Enlai of Communist China angered Russia by laying a wreath at Stalin's tomb.

After the split with China, Russian leaders Khruschev and Mikoyan began to feel the Chinese Communists led by Mao were a burden.

John and Jackie Kennedy at a White House reception.

Troubles for de Gaulle in Algeria

FRENCH PRESIDENT GENERAL DE GAULLE, faced increased problems in Algeria, where the Muslim majority opposed French rule. The French army had been fighting the Muslims for seven years. De Gaulle realized the French could not win and decided to discuss Algerian independence with the Muslims. On 23 April four French generals in the capital, Algiers, revolted. They hoped to get de Gaulle to change his mind, or even to get the army in France to revolt. They failed on both counts and on 25 April they gave in. Three of the generals were arrested, but their leader escaped to form the Secret Army Organization (OAS). On Friday 8 September the OAS tried to kill de Gaulle, setting off a bomb as he drove to his home near Paris, but de Gaulle escaped unharmed.

Congo crisis grows worse

FURTHER SOUTH IN AFRICA, the Congo crisis grew worse. The Katanga break-away continued, with General Mobutu holding Lumumba prisoner. Lumumba still had many followers, so to get rid of him Mobutu sent him to Katanga. There he was murdered by his enemies in February. The UN decided to back the national government against both the followers of Lumumba and the Katanga break away. In March, Lumumba followers gave up their fight against the national government, but UN soldiers continued the war against the Katanga leader, Moise Tshombe. The suspicion of murder hung round the death of UN leader Dag Hammarskjold when, in September, his plane blew up on a visit to Katanga. By December, the UN forces had won control of Katanga's capital and the war was over – for the moment.

Campaign for nuclear disarmament hots up

THE BIGGEST STORY in British politics in 1961 was the continuing argument about nuclear weapons. On 1 April 7000 people began marching from the nuclear weapons' base at Aldermaston in Berkshire to London to protest against the atom bomb. By 3 April 17,500 people had joined the march, which was nearing London. Marches of this kind had now been going for five years, however, and many 'Ban the Bomb' people were tired of waiting. They began non-violent direct action, led by the Committee of 100.

On 1 May, the Committee organized a sit-down demonstration in Whitehall. Eight hundred people were arrested and the philosopher, Bertrand Russell, sent a telegram of support to the demonstrators. Attention then switched to Scotland, where American nuclear submarines were based in Holy Loch. A demonstration took place on three piers at the base, and 41 people were arrested for obstruction. In September, a huge sit-down was planned for Parliament Square in London, and members of the Committee of 100 were arrested by the authorities. Lord and Lady Russell, playwright Arnold Wesker, and 30 other members of the Committee were sent to prison for refusing to be bound over. The prison sentences did not stop the sit-downs. On 18 September, 351 people were arrested for sitting down at Holy Loch. At the same time, 12,000 people sat down in Trafalgar Square and 1314 were arrested.

The Bay of Pigs

MEANWHILE, HOSTILITY between the United States and Cuba grew worse. On 4 January the Americans broke off diplomatic relations when the Cubans expelled all but 11 staff at the American embassy. Then, on 17 April, an American-backed invasion of Cuba by anti-Communist exiles took place. Several hundred exiles landed at the Bay of Pigs, having sailed from Florida. If the exiles believed that Cubans would rise against Castro they were wrong. After three days the invasion collapsed, with 350 exiles captured by Castro's government.

Labour backs the bomb

DESPITE THE DEMONSTRATIONS, the Labour Party reversed its support for nuclear disarmament. Some big unions which had backed the idea in 1960 changed their minds. Though the big Transport and General Workers Union voted again in favour of disarmament, the Engineering Union and the General and Municipal Workers Union decided to support the leader of the Labour Party, Hugh Gaitskell, who was in favour of Britain having the bomb. The Trades Union Congress backed the Labour leader at its conference in September, and on 4 October the Labour Party decided to switch its policy and back Britain having the bomb.

'A victory for fascists'

THE TORIES, meanwhile, had a quiet year. They did, however, make a very controversial move when, in November, they introduced a law limiting the right of Commonwealth citizens to come to live and work in Britain. Many people saw this as giving in to racism, and Hugh Gaitskell called it 'a victory for fascists'.

Sport and the Arts

Theatre

THE FLOW OF GOOD NEW BRITISH PLAYS and fine young actors continued in 1961. In March, N.F. Simpson's surreal play, *One-Way Pendulum*, had its first performance, and a new Simpson play, *Big Soft Nelly*, was seen in the autumn. Later in March, the Royal Shakespeare Theatre announced plans to stage a new play by Peter Shanffer, *The Royal Hunt of the Sun*. This was a brilliant work about the Spanish invasion of the Aztecs in Mexico. The Royal Shakespeare Theatre had a scheme to encourage new plays by young dramatists. John Arden, John Whiting, and Robert Bolt, whose play *A Man For All Seasons* had been such a success in 1960, were also part of the scheme. It was announced that Britain's best young actor, Albert Finney, was to give up the part of Billy Liar and play Luther in John Osborne's play about the German priest. Tom Courtney took over as Billy Liar, and did so well he later played the part in the film of the play.

Football highlights

1961 WAS NOT A GREAT YEAR for sport, but there were two memorable events in football. The great winger, Stanley Matthews, rejoined Second Division Stoke City in October, the club where he had begun his career, in 1930, as an apprentice. Big crowds turned up to see the veteran in the last matches of his career. More sensational was the achievement of Tottenham Hotspur in carrying off the FA Cup and League double. They were the first club to do this in the twentieth century, and many people believe they were the best team ever to play in the English First Division.

Best-sellers

MANY GOOD NEW BOOKS WERE PUBLISHED in 1961. In Britain, Iris Murdoch wrote *A Severed Head*, Graham Greene published *A Burnt-Out Case*, and Muriel Spark wrote *The Prime of Miss Jean Brodie*. In America, J.D. Salinger wrote *Franny and Zooey*, but the most important book of the year was the best-seller by Joseph Heller, *Catch 22*. This was another war book, about Americans fighting in Italy in the Second World War. Unlike most war books, it did not try to pretend fighting is glamorous or exciting. Instead, Heller wrote a book showing war as a crazy business run by crazy people. It sold over five million copies and was later made into a film.

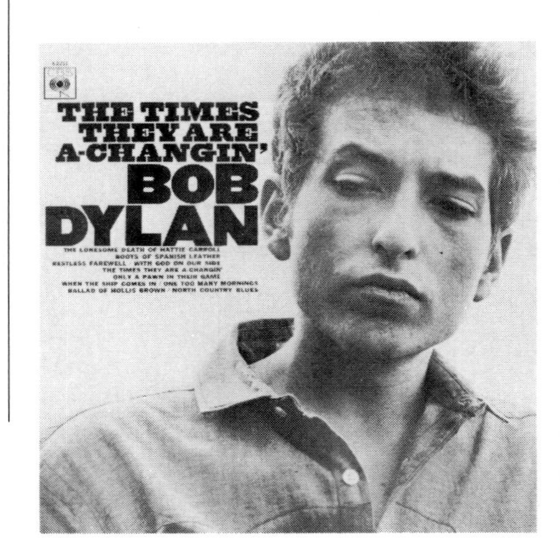

In 1961, Bob Dylan first made an impact on the American folk music scene.

The British film industry

THE FLOW OF GOOD BRITISH PLAYS AND BOOKS helped the British film industry. In February Willis Hall's play *The Long, the Short and the Tall*, was made into a film. In March, director Tony Richardson started to make a film of *A Taste of Honey*, Shelagh Delaney's play about young lovers. War films had an impact. In April, the world première of *The Guns of Navarone* took place, and in June work on the D-Day film *The Longest Day* was started.

Bob Dylan hits the US folk music scene

IN 1961 BOB DYLAN made his first record. The New York *Times* folk critic, Stacey Williams, wrote:

Excitement has been running high since the young man with a guitar ambled into a recording studio for two sessions in November 1961. For at only 20, Dylan is the most unusual new talent in American folk music. . . . He is one of the most compelling white blues singers ever recorded. He is a songwriter of exceptional facility and cleverness. In less than one year in New York, Bob Dylan has thrown the folk crowd into an uproar. Ardent fans have been shouting his praises. Devotees have found in him the image of a singing rebel, a musical Chaplin tramp, a young Woody Guthrie [veteran American folk singer], or a composite of some of the best country blues singers.

(Liner notes to CBS LP 'Bob Dylan', BPG 62022)

Man in space

IN 1961, SOVIET SCIENTISTS achieved one of the greatest triumphs in space exploration, when they launched a man into space. Both America and Russia had been preparing for this for some time by sending up animals. America sent a chimpanzee 155 miles into space in February, but this was completely overshadowed on the morning of 12 April, when the Russians sent a rocket into space carrying a 27-year-old cosmonaut, Yuri Gagarin. He spent 108 minutes in orbit round the world in a 4½-ton capsule, and at the highest point he had been 187 miles above the earth. Gagarin's craft returned by parachute, landing in central Russia. The Russians were delighted, and two days later Gagarin appeared with the Russian premier, Krushchev, in Moscow.

After his flight Gagarin was interviewed by the Soviet News Agency, TASS:

I was concentrating entirely on carrying out the programme of the flight. I wanted to carry out every part of the assignment and do it as well as possible. There was a lot of work. I well knew that my friends, the entire Soviet people, were following my space flight. I was sure that the Party and the Government would always be ready to help me if I found myself in difficulties. . .

We shall welcome the successs of the American cosmonauts. There is room in space for everybody. Space should be used for peaceful not military purposes. The American cosmonauts will have to catch up with us. We shall welcome their successes, but we shall try to be always ahead.

THE AMERICANS RUSHED AHEAD with their programme to get a man into space. On 29 April they tested the Mercury capsule, and on 5 May they sent Commander Alan Shephard into space in it. The capsule was fired by a Redstone rocket but this was not as powerful as the Russian rocket. Although Alan Shephard went 115 miles into space, he came down only 302 miles from the start point and the flight lasted only 15 minutes. It was a great achievement, but it wasn't as impressive as Gagarin's flight.

Yuri Gagarin in the cosmonaut's suit used in his flight.

Goonhilly Down gets space satellite station

DURING 1961 PROGRESS was made in attempts to use space satellites to send radio messages round the world. On 16 May, a special station to receive the signals was announced for Goonhilly Down in Cornwall in preparation for the Telstar satellite due in 1962.

Abu Simbel to be raised

IN JUNE IT WAS ANNOUNCED that an Italian plan to raise the ancient temple of Abu Simbel had been accepted by the Egyptian government. The temple, over 3000 years old, was due to be covered by a man-made lake. The Italian plan was to raise the temple, weighing over 150,000 tons, above the water. The project would cost £25 million and take eight years.

Medical achievements

IN OCTOBER – a patient undergoing an operation had his heart stopped for 82 minutes without damage to his brain. This was achieved by cooling the blood. The greatest scientific breakthrough of the year, however, was the discovery of the DNA molecule by the scientists Crick and Watson. DNA controls inheritance from one human generation to the next, and its discovery was a vital step forward for biological science.

The world's first jump jet

BRITISH AERO-ENGINEERS REVEALED the invention of the world's first jump jet, the Hawker P1127. In America, the X15 rocket plane reached 4070 m.p.h.

1962 The world

TUESDAY
OCTOBER 23, 1962
THREEPENCE
No. 14503

Daily Herald

All-ships ban on arms

KENNEDY BLOCKADES CUBA

A CUBAN BLOCKADE . . MIDNIGHT FLASHPOINT

Kennedy's blockade of Cuba made front-page headlines all over the world.

US spy plane photo shows a missile site in Cuba.

Kennedy v. Kruschev

In 1962 the world came closer to nuclear war than ever before or since. The flashpoint was Cuba. The United States had cut off trade and had asked her NATO allies to do the same, to help bring down the Castro government. As the Cubans became isolated they turned more and more to the Soviet Union for help. The Soviets took advantage of this to move missiles into Cuba from July onwards. From Cuba, missiles could be fired easily at the United States in time of war.

The Americans regarded missiles on an island only 90 miles off their coast as an unacceptable threat. A U2 spy plane flew over Cuba in October and photographed missiles in place – the first real evidence. On Tuesday 16 October, John Kennedy was shown the pictures, and the President formed a special group of advisers. Some advisers wanted to invade Cuba, others wanted to bomb the missiles. Both acts would have meant war with Russia. On Saturday 20 October the President decided as a first step to stop further rockets being sent to Cuba. He ordered the American navy to stop all Soviet ships taking missiles to Cuba. If the Soviet ships refused to stop when ordered to by American warships the Americans would sink them. Nevertheless, on Monday 22 October, the President announced a naval blockade 500 miles around Cuba, to start at 10 a.m. on Wednesday morning. As that time approached, two Soviet merchant ships were only miles off the limit, protected by a Soviet submarine. The atmosphere in the President's office was tense. If a battle between the Soviet submarine and American warships began, this could be the start of the Third World War.

on the brink

Geared for war

DRAMATICALLY, JUST BEFORE the Soviet ships reached the limit, they stopped and turned back. This was not the end of the matter. Kennedy wrote to Premier Kruschev asking him to remove the missiles. Kruschev refused and told the Americans their naval blockade was useless as the Russians already had enough missiles in Cuba to attack the United States. The President's advisers knew this, and urged him to bomb the missiles. Kennedy refused, hoping that Kruschev would agree to remove the rockets in exchange for American promises to call off the blockade and not to invade Cuba.

While waiting for the Russian reply to this offer, Kennedy ordered preparations for an air attack on Cuba. Twenty-four squadrons of the air force reserve were called up, and Washington prepared for war. Then, on Sunday 28 October, Kennedy received a letter from Kruschev agreeing to take the rockets out of Cuba if the United States promised not to invade the island. The Americans did so, and the crisis was over.

After the Cuban Crisis was over, brinkmanship was praised, but it was dangerous.

Protest develops

MANY AMERICANS BACKED Kennedy's tough Cuban stand, even though it risked a Third World War, but some were shocked by how near nuclear war had come. The crisis strengthened the growing protest song movement and produced strong comments from writers like Phil Ochs:

TALKING CUBA INVASION

Yes, it seemed the stand was strong and plain
But some Republicans were going insane (and they still are)
They said our plan was much too mild
Spare the rod and spoil the child
Sink Cuba back into the sea
Give them back democracy (Yes, under the water)

Independents call for peace

MEANWHILE, THE NON-ALIGNED NATIONS – countries not linked to either Russia or America – were appalled by the actions of the Superpowers.

At their conference, in Belgrade, Yugoslavia, on 27 September, they issued a strong appeal for peace. They said it was

urgent and imperative that the parties concerned, more particularly the USA and USSR should immediately suspend their military preparations and resume negotiations for a peaceful settlement of outstanding differences between them . . . and continue negotiating until both they and the rest of the world achieve total disarmament and enduring peace.

They appealed to Kennedy and Kruschev to make immediate and direct approaches to each other to avert the imminent conflict and establish peace.

Kruschev faces critics

RUSSIA'S BACKDOWN OVER CUBA angered the Chinese, who saw it as another sign that Russia was letting down the Communist cause. The quarrel between the two countries grew worse as the nomads in western China fought the Chinese army, then fled into Russia, where they were welcomed. When war broke out between China and India in October 1962, Russia, far from backing their fellow Communists, criticized China as posing a threat to world peace.

Under Joseph Stalin, all Communist countries had followed the policies laid down in Moscow, but the Communists were now split. This was shown again when the leaders of Communist Albania were welcomed in Peking – even though the Soviet leaders in Moscow had broken off links with Albania the previous year.

Winds of change in Africa

IN AFRICA, some problems were solved while others grew worse. In Algeria the seven-year-long war came to an end in March when a ceasefire was organized between the French and the Muslim Algerian majority. The Secret Army Organization (OAS) formed a resistance group to continue fighting to keep Algeria linked to France, but in July the country became independent. Attempts by the OAS to 'punish' the people they believed had betrayed French Algeria were the basis for Frederick Forsyth's book *The Day of the Jackal*.

Events in the newly independent Central African Federation were moving towards a break up. The all-white Rhodesian Front led by Ian Smith was voted into power in Southern Rhodesia against Sir Roy Welensky. Smith promised to maintain white rule against the black majority. In December, Nyasaland, under its new black majority government, left the Federation and it was clear the Federation was not working.

In South Africa, repression of apartheid protestors continued with the arrest of African leader Nelson Mandela, on 5 August. On 7 November he was sentenced to five years in prison for trying to organize a general strike. In early 1988, he had still not been released.

Nelson Mandela prior to imprisonment.

Cartoonist Vicky drew Macmillan as Britannia, wooing President de Gaulle for marriage between Britain and France in the Common Market.

American presence in Vietnam increased

FIGHTING BETWEEN THE CHINESE-BACKED COMMUNIST VIETCONG guerillas and the American-backed South Vietnamese government escalated in 1962. By the end of the year there were 16,500 American troops in Vietnam. Government casualties numbered 14,000 that year, as compared with 4900 in 1960.

Supermac faces problems

IN 1962, TORY PRIME MINISTER Harold Macmillan's reputation as a master problem-solver had a setback. His government was shocked when it lost an MP at a by-election in the London suburb of Orpington in March. A Tory majority of more then 14,000 was turned into a Liberal majority of 7855 as Eric Lubbock won an unexpected victory. This was the first example of a protest vote. A large number of Tories, unhappy with the Conservative government, voted Liberal and, together with some ex-Labour voters, managed to send a Liberal to Parliament.

Macmillan also faced problems abroad. An important change in Britain's world position took place during the summit conference held between Macmillan and American President John Kennedy in Nassau in December. The British, having abandoned plans to build their own Blue Streak guided missile, had made arrangements to buy the American Skybolt air-launched rocket. The Americans then decided to opt instead for the Polaris submarine-launched missile. Macmillan agreed that the British would buy this, showing that the British depended on the United States for their missiles. Although the atomic war-heads were still made in Britain, many people said the British bomb was not a really independent weapon. The French claimed that Britain was too closely tied to the United States.

De Gaulle used this argument to keep Britain out of the European Economic Community (EEC). British claims to a 'Special Relationship' with the Americans, however, suffered a blow when Kennedy offered Polaris to the French. The French refused. Meanwhile, De Gaulle continued to try to heal the long-standing emnity between France and Germany. De Gaulle and Chancellor Ardenauer exchanged state visits.

Commonwealth Immigrants bill

THE MOST IMPORTANT DECISION of the British Parliament in 1962 was to pass the Commonwealth Immigration Bill, restricting the number of immigrants from the New Commonwealth who were allowed to enter the country. Previously, all Commonwealth citizens had had a British passport, and thus the right to enter Britain.

Kitchen sink and satire

IN THE ARTS IN BRITAIN, the fashion of depicting the lives of ordinary people as realistically as possible continued. In the theatre, Arnold Wesker's play *Chips with Everything* showed life in an RAF camp as lived by rank-and-file airmen. In the cinema, John Schlesinger's film *A Kind of Loving* dramatized Stan Barstow's novel of the same name. This was about a couple who, having married because the woman is pregnant, find they have to make their marriage work even though they are not really in love.

This kind of honest treatment of a subject previously too sensitive to be discussed was typical of British art at this time. In February, the crime series 'Z-Cars' began on television. This showed policemen as ordinary human beings, capable of making mistakes. The police did not like this kind of presentation of the force, and the Chief Constable of Lancashire, where the series was set, travelled to London to protest to the BBC. He was swimming against the tide. Though most programmes were sympathetic to the police (crime was a very popular subject on television, with series like 'M-Squad' and 'The Naked City', and the American imports 'Danger Man', '77 Sunset Strip', and 'Perry Mason'), this was the year when the satire boom began, with its idea of poking fun at authority. The magazine *Private Eye*, the television programme 'That Was The Week That Was', and comics in night clubs found a ready audience for jokes about public figures.

Freedom movement

THE MOVEMENT FOR MORE FREEDOM was running strong. A sign of the times was the decision made in February by the students at Oxford University to let women into the previously all-male students union. Even the Catholic Church, usually very keen to lay down strict rules for its followers, was touched. On 11 October the Vatican Council opened in St Peter's Church in Rome, and many people, both inside and outside the Catholic Church, hoped that this very powerful religious body would allow more freedom for its followers (e.g. accepting modern methods of birth control). These hopes were not to be fulfilled, but in the atmosphere of 1962 they were not far-fetched.

Pop takes a turn

DURING 1962 – pop music was dominated by Elvis Presley, Cliff Richard and wholesome, middle-of-the-road, short-haired music. Typical of the mainstream was 'Telstar', an instrumental by the Tornadoes inspired by the space satellite. This topped the chart on both sides of the Atlantic, then the Tornadoes vanished from sight.

In America, folk protest attracted teenagers bored with this musical diet. In Britain, there were two developments. In and around London, the fashion was for 'rhythm and blues'. In Liverpool and the North, the groups were turning to hard 'rock and roll'. Very little notice was taken by the press of either of these movements, and when in October a new Liverpool group issued its first record, few people paid much attention. The record was 'Love Me Do' and the group was the Beatles.

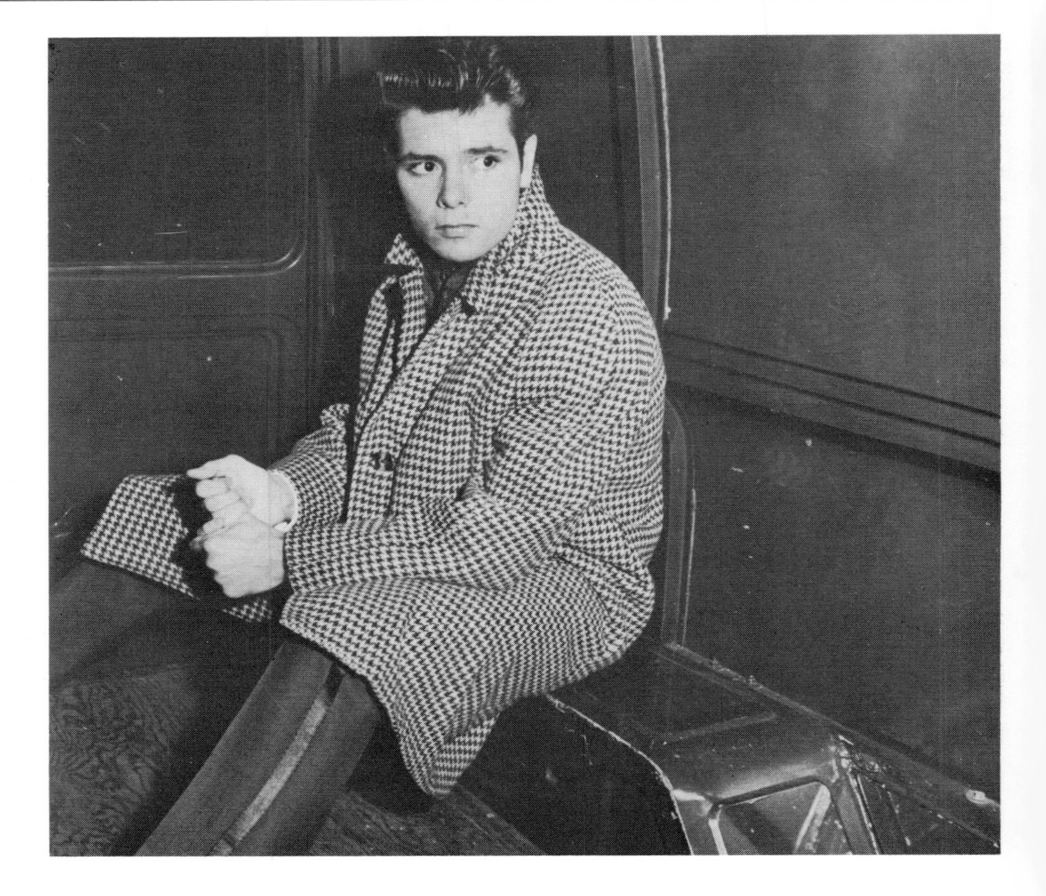

Cliff Richard.

Co-operation in space

1962 WAS A YEAR of important developments in space exploration. The United States finally managed to put a man, Colonel John Glenn, into orbit round the earth on 20 February. After the flight, the Russians invited the Americans to co-operate in space. Kruschev wrote to Kennedy, saying:

If our countries pooled their efforts – scientific, technical and material – to explore outer space, this would be very beneficial to the advance of science and would be acclaimed by all peoples who wish to see scientific achievements benefit man and not be used for 'Cold War' purposes and the arms race.

Kennedy welcomed this as 'most encouraging', replying:

We believe that when men reach beyond this planet they should leave their national differences behind them. All men will benefit if we can invoke the wonders of science instead of its terrors. . . We will indicate in response our desire that space be explored peacefully [and] that we will be prepared to discuss this matter at the UN, or bilaterally.

The worsening relations between the Superpowers over Cuba did not entirely stop this co-operation.

Polaris v. Skybolt

ELSEWHERE, THE DEVELOPMENT of the Polaris submarine-launched, nuclear-armed rocket, and the abandoning of the aircraft-launched Skybolt missile, showed that in a nuclear war it would be rockets and not aircraft which would prove the most devastating weapons.

Messages around the world

PROBABLY THE MOST IMPORTANT development in the peaceful use of space, however, was the successful launching of the world's first telecommunications satellite, Telstar. This was launched by the United States in July. Described as 'a sapphire-studded object about the size and shape of a beach ball', it was able to transmit messages from one continent to another at the speed of light. 34½ in. (88 cm) in diameter, and weighing 170 lb [77 kg], it had an orbit ranging from 593 miles from the earth to 3502 miles at its farthest point. It had cost £17 million. On 19 July it broadcast press reports from New York to London, and on 23 July the first live television programmes from Europe to America and vice versa.

Economic warnings

FOR MOST PEOPLE IN BRITAIN, life remained prosperous and satisfying. There were clear signs, however, that the British economy was running into problems and that it was failing to compete with newer industries abroad. The British ship-building industry, for example, was still the second most important in the world in 1962 – it built nearly 1.7 million tons as against the two million tons built in Japan. However, the British were not as quick or as cheap as the Japanese, and a headline in February read 'Britain is losing the battle against Japanese shipbuilders'. It was a sign of things to come.

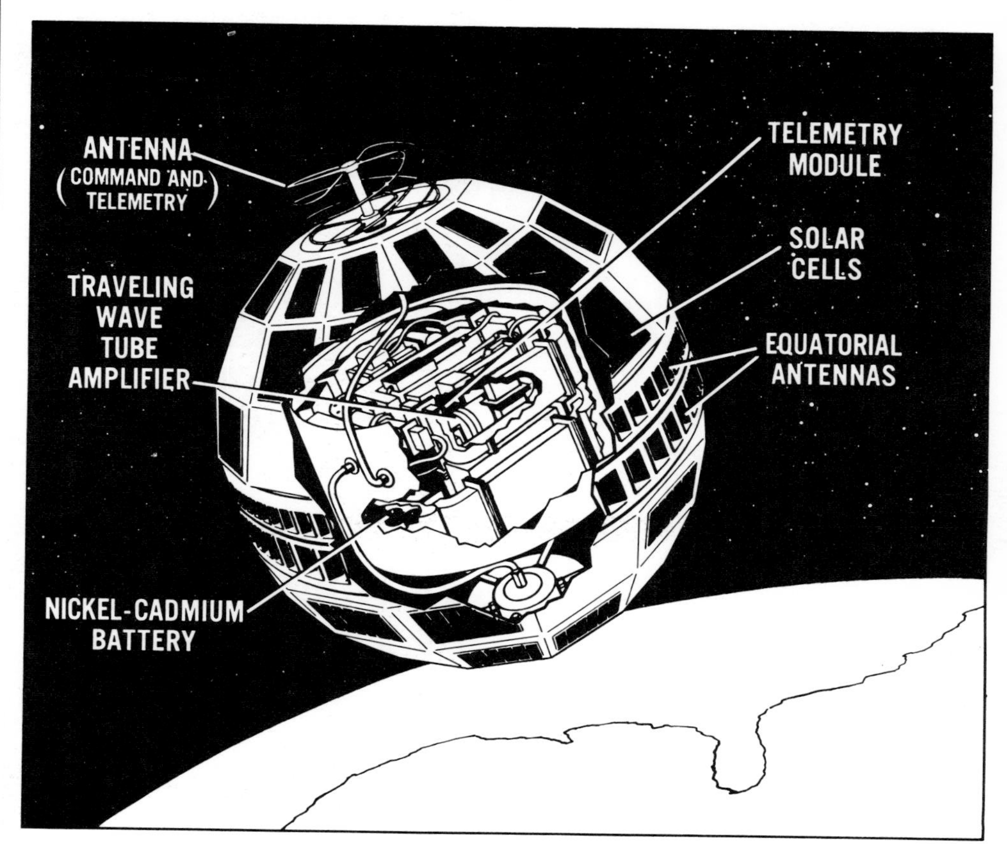

Telstar in a cut-away maker's diagram.

1963 The death

Daily Mirror

KENNEDY ASSASSINATED

3d. Saturday, November 23, 1963 No. 18,640

Jackie spattered with blood

Mrs. Kennedy, her clothes spattered with blood, bends over her dying husband as their car races to hospital.

Kennedy's assassination shocked the world.

Kennedy's enemies

KENNEDY HAD BEEN a controversial President. Many Americans opposed his support for black people, while others were angry at his failure to kick the Communists out of Cuba. The extreme right wing had threatened to kill him, but no one took these threats seriously. Kennedy had been warned it was dangerous to drive through the streets of Dallas in an open car, but he felt that the President had to be able to drive openly anywhere in the country, and few people expected trouble.

Kennedy hit by gunman's bullet

ON 22 NOVEMBER, as Kennedy drove slowly through crowd-lined streets of Dallas in an open car, together with his wife, Jackie, and Governor Connally of Texas, three or more shots were fired at the car. Kennedy was shot through the throat and head, and Governor Connally was also hit. The President's driver immediately raced for the Parkland hospital, with Jackie Kennedy, covered in her husband's blood, cradling her husband's head. John Kennedy was unconscious and never woke again. He was still alive when he was admitted to the hospital, but two Catholic priests were called to administer the last rites, and Kennedy died at 2 p.m. It was 35 minutes after the shots had been fired. A doctor said, 'We never had any chance of saving his life'.

When they arrived at Love Field . . . the President, disembarking, walked immediately across the sunlit field to the crowd and shook hands. Then they entered the cars to drive from the airport to the centre of the city. . . The car turned off Main Street, the President happy and waving, Jacqueline erect and proud by his side, and Mrs Connally saying, 'You certainly can't say that the people of Dallas haven't given you a nice welcome', and the automobile turning on to Elm Street and down the slope past the Texas School Book Depository, and the shots, faint and frightening, suddenly distinct over the roar of the motorcade, and the quizzical look on the President's face before he pitched over, and Jacqueline crying, 'Oh, no, no. . . Oh, my God, they have shot my husband', and the horror, the vacancy.

Arthur M Schlesinger, Special Assistant to President Kennedy, in *A Thousand Days: John F. Kennedy in the White House*, 1965

# of a President

A double murder hunt

THE POLICE SEARCHED the Texas Book Depository building, from where the shots seemed to come, and on the sixth floor found a rifle with telescopic sights. The search for the killer became a double murder hunt when a policeman, Officer Tippit, was shot challenging a man acting suspiciously. Shortly after, police arrested a man named Lee Harvey Oswald, who worked in the Book Depository. Police claimed his palm print and finger prints had been found on and near the rifle. Tests showed traces of gun shot on his hands. Nevertheless, Oswald denied he had killed either John Kennedy or Officer Tippit.

On Saturday, 23 November, Oswald was questioned again by police but continued to deny the killings. On Sunday, the police decided to move Oswald to the county jail. There had been several phone calls threatening Oswald's life, but the move was well publicized. As Oswald left the building, a Dallas night club owner, Jack Ruby, slipped through the waiting crowd and fired a pistol at Oswald at point blank range. Oswald died almost immediately. Ruby was arrested and later said, 'I didn't want to be a hero, I did it for Jacqueline Kennedy'.

Lee Harvey Oswald

A 24-YEAR-OLD ex-Marine, trained to use guns, Oswald was an extreme left winger, not a right winger as many had feared. He had defected to the USSR, then returned and become chair of the local Fair Play for Cuba Committee.

America mourns its President

AMERICA WAS OVERCOME by grief and shock. People cried in the streets as they heard about the President's death on television and radio. The judge hearing Vice President Lyndon Johnson swearing the oath which made him the new President of the United States, cried as she did so. When the shock subsided, however, questions remained. Did Oswald really kill the President? Was there only one killer? A film-maker at the scene of the crime claimed to have filmed another gunman. Was Oswald a Communist acting under orders? Why had he been to Virginia and Mexico recently? How could Jack Ruby kill Oswald so easily? These and other questions were to be investigated by the Warren Commission in 1964.

Comments on Kennedy's death

FUNERAL ORATION, Justice Earl Warren:

John Fitzgerald Kennedy, a great and good President, the friend of all men of goodwill, has been snatched from our midst by the bullet of an assassin. What moved some misguided wretch to do this horrible deed may never be known to us, but we do know that such acts are commonly stimulated by forces of hatred and malevolence, such as are today eating their way into the bloodstream of American life. . . . Is it too much to hope that the martyrdom of our beloved President might even soften the hearts of those who would themselves recoil from assassination, but who do not shrink from spreading the venom which kindles thoughts of it in others?

Fidel Castro:

The death of a man, even though he is our enemy, cannot be cause for jubilation. We Cubans must . . . not confuse systems with the individual. We fight against systems, not against the man.

The first televised murder: Ruby shoots Oswald.

US – Soviet relations improve

RELATIONS BETWEEN THE UNITED STATES and the Soviet Union improved in 1963. The United States considered an air blockade of Cuba in January, and restricted American shipping to Cuba in February, but Russia agreed to remove her troops from the island. On 4 April, Kennedy reported that 5000 Soviet troops had left the previous November, 4000 that March, and that Russia had promised to withdraw the remaining 13,000. A hotline was set up between Moscow and Washington in April, and in October the United States sold wheat to Russia. On 25 July, Russia, America and Britain signed a treaty to ban atom tests above ground.

Kennedy and civil rights

ONE REASON WHY John Kennedy was so unpopular with the right wing was his support for black civil rights. The black campaign for equal rights with whites was well under way – even though white racists opposed it with violence. On 31 January, James Meredith, the first black man at the University of Mississippi, agreed to go back for a second term, even though he had to be guarded night and day against murder threats. On 29 March, 11 people leading a drive to get blacks the vote in Greenwood, Mississippi, were arrested, two shotgun blasts were fired into the home of a black man, and the HQ of the black votes campaign was burnt down.

On 12 June the President sent a Civil Right Bill to Congress, which, if passed, would make equality a legal right. On 28 August between 100,000 and 200,000 black people, led by Martin Luther King, marched in Washington in support of the Civil Rights Bill. But the violence did not stop. In September, a black man was shot dead in Alabama, four blacks were killed when a church in Birmingham, Alabama, was bombed, Medgar Evers of the National Association for the Advancement of Coloured People was murdered, and six black children were killed when a house was burnt down.

Martin Luther King at the march on Washington.

Religious divisions in South Vietnam

PRESIDENT DIEM and his government were Catholics, but 70 per cent of the population of South Vietnam was Buddhist. Trouble between the two groups increased and America warned she would pull her troops out of Vietnam if matters were not settled. In October she stopped sending aid to the unpopular Diem government. In November the South Vietnamese army rebelled against Diem and he and his brother were killed. The USA was believed to have backed the army.

Change of leadership in Britain

IN 1963 IN BRITAIN, both Labour and Tory Parties changed leaders. In January, Hugh Gaitskell was suddenly taken ill, and on 19 January he died. Harold Wilson was then elected leader of the Labour Party. Harold Macmillan seemed certain to lead the Tory Party into the next election, but after a prostate operation he resigned on 11 October. Lord Alec Douglas Home was appointed leader of the Tory Party and Prime Minister on 19 October.

France says 'No' to Britain joining EEC

IT HAD BEEN A BAD YEAR for the Tories. The French had opposed the British application to join the Common Market, arguing that Britain was 'not ready' for the EEC, as she was still too friendly with the USA. On 29 January 1964, the French stopped talks on the British application.

The Profumo affair

THE TORIES HAD an even worse shock over the Profumo affair. In March, Labour MPs asked about rumours involving a Cabinet minister and a Miss Keeler. On 22 March the Minister for War, John Profumo – one of the top ministers in the government – announced that he was the minister concerned, but that there was nothing wrong with his knowing Miss Keeler, and that he had not seen her since December 1961:

I understand that my name has been connected with the rumours about the disappearance of Miss Keeler. I would like to take this opportunity of making a personal statement about these matters. I last saw Miss Keeler in December 1961, and I have not seen her since. . . Between July and December 1961 I met Miss Keeler on about half a dozen occasions . . . Miss Keeler and I were on friendly terms. There was no impropriety whatsoever in my acquaintanceship with Miss Keeler. . .
Profumo's statement to the House, 22 March 1963.

On 6 June, Profumo resigned from the government, after sensationally admitting he had lied:

On 22 March I made a personal statement. Rumour had charged me with assisting in the disappearance of a witness. . . . I allowed myself to think that my personal association with that witness . . . was of minor importance. . . . In my statement I said that there had been no impropriety in this association. To my very deep regret, I have to admit that this was not true, and that I misled you, and my colleagues, and the House. . .
Profumo's statement to the House, 5 June 1963.

He admitted he had been having an affair with Christine Keeler. Moreover, Christine Keeler was a prostitute run by a high-class pimp, Stephen Ward, and had also had a relationship with Captain Eugene Ivanov, Assistant Naval Attaché at the Soviet Embassy. It was immediately suspected that the Russians had been using Keeler to get secrets out of Profumo.

John Profumo, the Minister, and Christine Keeler, his downfall.

This was never proved, but a sensational story of corruption in high places emerged. Stephen Ward was a doctor, treating only the rich and famous – people such as Winston Churchill, Paul Getty and Elizabeth Taylor. He was an artist who had drawn the Duke of Edinburgh, Princess Margaret and Lord Snowden, as well as other members of the Royal Family. Yet this friend of the rich and royalty was arrested on 10 June and charged with living off immoral earnings.

On 1 August Stephen Ward was found guilty on two charges. He was not in court, having been rushed to hospital after an overdose of drugs. He died 80 hours later. The sensations did not end there. On 6 December Christine Keeler was sentenced to nine months in gaol for perjury. The fact that Macmillan had not known his War Minister was involved with the Ward circle seemed astonishing to many people.

British news headlines

- CND supporters, called Spies for Peace, stated where government headquarters for a nuclear war were sited.
- Britain's crime of the century, the Great Train Robbery, took place. A Post Office train was stopped and robbed of £2½ million.
- The government passed a bill allowing lords to give up their peerages. Labour Lord Tony Wedgwood Benn and Tory Lord Alec Douglas Home both did so and became MPs.

Boxing

BOXING PROVIDED the main sporting story of the year with the world heavyweight championship dominated by two of the world's greatest ever boxers – Sonny Liston and Cassius Clay. Sonny Liston had sensationally beaten the previous champion, Floyd Patterson, with a knock-out in two minutes six seconds in September 1962. On 24 July 1963 Liston repeated his victory by flooring Patterson in two minutes ten seconds. He seemed so strong that no one could imagine him being beaten. But the 1960 Olympic light-heavyweight champion, Cassius Clay, was now a formidable heavyweight fighter. On 18 June, Clay beat Britain's champion, Henry Cooper in just five rounds, and boxing fans eagerly awaited a fight between Clay and Liston.

Cassius Clay and Henry Cooper, looking a little the worse for wear, after their contest at Wembley.

Beatles top the charts

THE BEATLES, with songs like 'Please Please Me', 'She Loves You', 'From Me to You', and a string of other hits were the pop phenomenon of the year in Britain. On 5 December the Beatles took part in the Royal Variety Performance, and even *The Times* newspaper wrote about them.

The lovable mop-tops: the Beatles in 1963.

If I Had a Hammer

If I had a hammer, I'd hammer in the morning,
I'd hammer in the evening, all over this land,
I'd hammer out justice! I'd hammer out a warning!
I'd hammer out the love between my brothers and my sisters,
All over this land. . .

Written by Pete Seeger, recorded by Trini Lopez; reached Number 1 in the US hit parade in the last week of August 1963.

A modern ballet

IN DECEMBER THE BRITISH WESTERN THEATRE BALLET produced a modern ballet – 'Mods and Rockers' – about two rival teenage cults. The mods – clean-cut, fashion-conscious kids on scooters, wearing collarless, high-button Beatles-style jackets and Chelsea boots – often fought with the motorbike gangs (rockers, or greasers), with their leather jackets and greased-back hair. The ballet told the story of a mod girl carried away by a rocker on a motorbike, and was set to Beatles' songs.

The US music scene

IN AMERICA, FOLK MUSIC was the big pop story of the year. The Kingston Trio and New Christie Minstrels had hits, while Trini Lopez took veteran protest writer Pete Seeger's 'If I Had a Hammer' into the top ten. The real action, though, was in the album rather than the single charts. At one point, Peter, Paul and Mary had three of the top five selling albums in the United States, and Bob Dylan outsold Tony Bennett. The protest scene was thriving. The underground magazine *Broadside* carried songs by dozens of writers across America, including Bob Dylan.

Films and books

1963 WAS ANOTHER memorable year for films. Harold Pinter showed he could write films as well as plays with the brilliant film *The Servant*. The American cinema produced two masterpieces of horror, *Whatever Happened to Baby Jane* and Hitchcock's *The Birds*. Hollywood produced a memorable war film, *The Great Escape*, and a less memorable spectacular, *Cleopatra*, with Stephen Ward's client, Elizabeth Taylor, in the title role. Polish film director Roman Polanski's thriller *Knife in the Water* marked the start of a remarkable career.

There were some fine books this year also, notably Alexander Solzhenitsyn's story of a Russian labour camp, *One Day in the Life of Ivan Denisovitch*, and Ken Kesey's American novel *One Flew over the Cuckoo's Nest*.

Supersonic flight

THE IDEA of a supersonic airliner was now being taken seriously. Following the decision in 1962 to build a joint British-French plane, the Concorde, the Americans decided in January 1963 to design a plane capable of speeds of up to 2500 m.p.h. In June the American airline, PanAm, provisionally ordered six Concordes. By December, the problems of sonic boom, the explosive sound caused by the shock wave of planes flying at super-sonic speeds, were being discussed.

Limited co-operation in space

FOLLOWING COLONEL JOHN GLENN'S flight round the earth in 1962 America and Russia had agreed in principle to work together on space exploration. On 16 August the American National Aeronautics and Space Administration and the Soviet Academy of Sciences announced detailed plans for co-operation on weather and communication satellites. There was to be joint work on weather experiments and in radio communication via the American Echo balloon satellite.

Despite this, the arms race between the two countries continued. On the forty-fifth anniversary of the Red Army the Soviet Union claimed that it could now launch rockets from space satellites, and had had an intercontinental missile able to deliver a 100-megaton warhead. Marshal Malinovsky warned that if the USA attacked the USSR,

We shall deal a blow . . . with such a tremendous nuclear yield that it will wipe off the face of the earth all targets, all industrial and administrative-political centres in the United States, and will completely destroy the countries which have made their territories available for American war bases.

This warning came after Kruschev had already announced that the new 100-megaton warhead – equivalent to 100 million tons of TNT – was so danger-ous that the USSR could not drop it on Western Europe without damaging her own allies. There was little room for complacency in world politics.

Foreign scientists and military experts estimate that the US now has roughly 40,000 hydrogen bombs and warheads. Everyone knows that the Soviet Union, too, has more than enough of this stuff. What would happen if all these nuclear warheads were brought down on people? Scientists estimate that the first blow alone would take a toll of 700 to 800 million lives. All the cities would be wiped out – not only in the two leading nuclear countries . . . but in France, Britain, Germany, Italy, China, Japan, and many other countries. . . .

On the 100-megaton bomb:
Soviet military chiefs are of the opinion that such a weapon could not be used in Europe if our probable adversary unleashes a war. Should such a bomb be dropped in Western Germany or France, for example, it would not only destroy these countries but also Eastern Germany . . . this weapon can be used by us, apparently, only outside Western Europe.
Kruschev's speech to the sixth Congress of the East German Communist Party, 16 January 1963

Progress in space

IN SPACE, the Soviets launched a fourth unmanned moon probe, Lunik IV. This missed the moon by 5300 miles, and the Soviets announced on 28 October that they would not try to send a human being to the moon. Instead, they concentrated on space satellites, and in June became the first country to send a woman into space.

In October the French sent a cat into space, and recovered it successfully.

The Americans, meanwhile, complained bitterly about poor work on their space satellites. Seven hundred and twenty faults had been found in the reserve spacecraft for their last mission, there had been defective wiring in Commander Glenn's capsule, and a total of $100 million worth of repairs had to be made.

Valentina Tereshkova, the first woman astronaut.

Nuclear sub sinks

THE DANGERS of even the most advanced technology were illustrated when the American nuclear submarine *Thresher* was declared overdue and missing on 11 April. A massive search was launched, but on 13 April it was announced that the submarine had sunk with the loss of all 129 crew members. Both the Russians and the Americans continued to build these very expensive boats, however. The Soviets had 26 nuclear submarines and the Americans 31. The USA planned to have 86 by 1968, and the USSR to build 12 per year indefinitely.

1964 America's

Khan seizes power in South Vietnam

THE SITUATION IN SOUTH VIETNAM hit the headlines more and more in 1964. At the end of January Major General Nguyen Khan seized power, but he failed to provide a strong or united leadership. Vietcong activity increased. The week of 15-22 January showed 412 incidents, whereas the average for 1963 had been 270 per week. Robert MacNamara, US Defence Secretary, said, 'The survival of an independent government in South Vietnam is so important . . . that I can conceive of no alternative other than to take all necessary measures within our capability to prevent a Communist victory'. America might want to beat the Communists, but could she do so?

On 24 February reports came in that the South Vietnamese army had refused to help hamlets being attacked by the Vietcong, especially at night. The man said to be responsible for the fall of Diem, Roger Hilsman, Assistant Secretary of State for Far Eastern Affairs, lost his job at the end of February; getting rid of Diem had made things worse for America. The new army government still had not gained the support of the Buddhist majority, who hated the Americans, and it was not easy to find trained administrators to run the government. The Americans were also losing an increasing number of men. By April an average of 91 US soldiers were dying in Vietnam per month. In 1963 it had been 42 per month. In May it was reported that American officers were reluctant to serve in Vietnam because they feared 'inevitable disaster'.

Ho Chi Minh, the deceptively bland leader of North Vietnam.

America increases support

AMERICA DECIDED TO INCREASE her support of South Vietnam. On 24 June General Maxwell Taylor took over as American ambassador in Saigon. Taylor was the leading US soldier, the chair of the Joint Chiefs of Staff. 'In recent Congressional evidence', it was reported, 'he has said that the war could be won with the necessary determination and effort'. In July, 5000 more American 'advisers' were sent to South Vietnam, making a total of more than 20,000.

Map published in the Daily Telegraph *showing the alleged second attack in the Gulf of Tonkin – later there was some doubt as to whether or not the incident had ever taken place.*

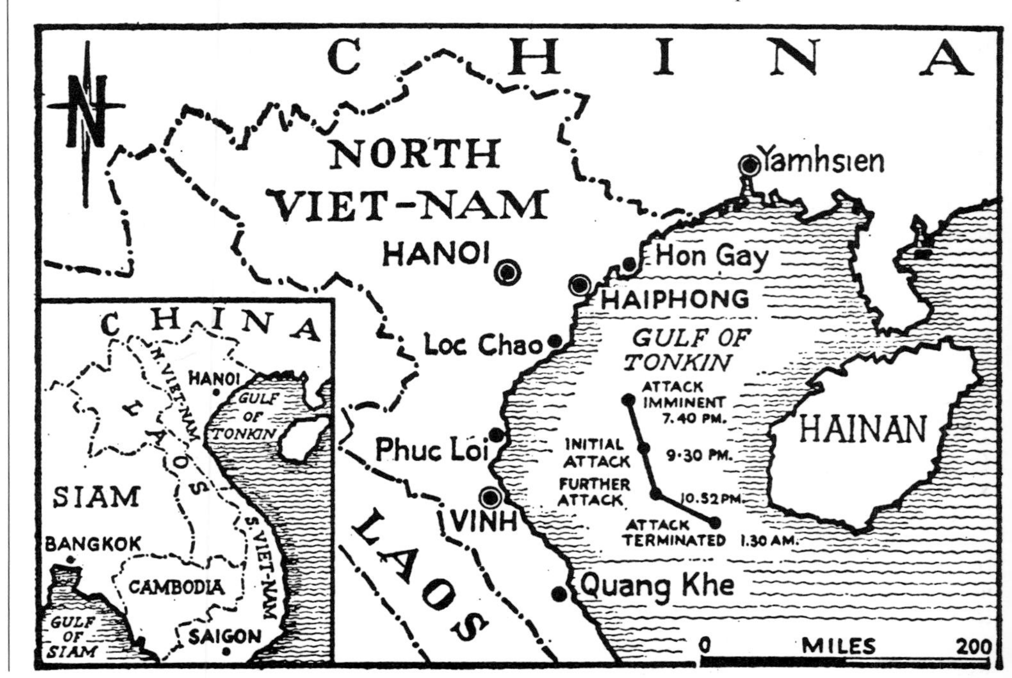

Asian war

Gulf of Tonkin incident

UP TO NOW, American troops in South Vietnam were only 'advisers', who were not allowed to take the offensive. This changed in August, after the so-called 'Gulf of Tonkin incident'. On 2 August the US destroyer *Maddox* was attacked by North Vietnamese gunboats after allegedly penetrating Vietnamese waters. There is no dispute that this happened. Then, on the night of 4 August, the Americans claimed that two destroyers had been attacked on the high seas in the Gulf of Tonkin. The President ordered US planes to bomb targets in North Vietnam, and America was now at war with the Hanoi government. But did the second incident ever take place? At the time, the Communists claimed the United States had invented the second attack to allow them to attack North Vietnam. Subsequent investigations suggest they may have been right.

As President and Commander-in-Chief, it is my duty to the American people to report that renewed hostile actions against US ships on the high seas in the Gulf of Tonkin have required me to order the military forces of the United States to take action in reply.

The initial attack on the destroyer 'Maddox', on Aug 2nd, was repeated today by a number of hostile vessels attacking two US destroyers with torpedoes. The destroyers, and supporting aircraft, acted at once on the orders I gave after the initial act of aggression. We believe at least two of the attacking boats were sunk. There were no US losses.

President Lyndon Johnson, television broadcast, 4 August 1964.

In fact, the so-called incident of Aug 4th did not occur. On that night the Democratic Republic of Vietnam did not have a single naval vessel in the waters where the US warships were. . . . The facts prove that this so-called incident is an out-and-out lie fabricated by US Imperialism in order to extend the war in Indo-China. . . . The bombing of coastal towns of the DRV on Aug 5th was a premeditated move by US Imperialism to extend the (Indo-China) war step by step. . . . The Chinese people will not stand idly by without lending a helping hand. The debt of blood incurred by the United States to the Vietnamese people must be repaid.

Official statement by Chinese government, Peking, 6 August 1964.

The terrible reality of the Vietnam War: a South Vietnamese woman pleads with an American soldier to save her home, which is blazing.

The South Vietnamese government

MORE AMERICAN SUPPORT could not solve the problems of the South Vietnamese government, however. On 16 August General Khan lost his job as chief of state to Major General Duong Van Minh, and late in August there were riots in Saigon. By 4 September Khan was reinstated as prime minister, and on 14 September there was an attempt to overthrow him. On 19 November Maxwell Taylor was recalled to Washington to discuss new plans, including attacking North Vietnam. More troops were sent; by the end of November 22,000 American soldiers were in South Vietnam. Mr Huong was now in charge of the government, but the Buddhists were still not supporting the war.

Could the US win in Vietnam?

ON 12 DECEMBER 1964 *The Times* carried the following article:

The American budget for Vietnam is $500 million (£179 million) a year, and there is little . . . to suggest it has done anything but delay eventual defeat. . . . The US can be said to have made . . . the classic error of identifying itself with a regime that does not have the support of much of the population. Perhaps the error was inevitable after the interference of the Kennedy administration which brought about the downfall and murder of Diem when clearly the Buddhist majority was unprepared to continue the association with the US.

Civil rights in the USA

In the USA, the problems of black people were often in the headlines. Lyndon Johnson continued to support the Civil Rights Movement, and on 12 February a Civil Rights Bill was passed through the House of Representatives by 290 votes to 130. US senators still had to vote in favour of the bill if it was to become law, and many senators opposed it. They tried to stop it by organizing a filibuster. This meant that they continued to debate the subject so that a vote could not be taken. The filibuster started on 10 March, and went on for weeks. Only after two months, on 11 May, did the majority of senators decide there had been enough talking, and voted 71 to 29 to end the debate. The Civil Rights Bill was then passed.

In the meantime, however, frustration had built up among both blacks and racist whites. Blacks felt no progress was being made to help them and resented the failure of the police to catch the murderers of black people. They began to take the law into their own hands. Rioting took place in Alabama in February and spread to Mississippi in March. During a long, hot summer, riots took place in New York, New Jersey and Philadelphia. Black violence sparked a white backlash. The racist governor of Alabama, George Wallace, campaigned to become the democratic candidate for the presidency. He had no chance against Lyndon Johnson, but even so, won much support.

After three civil rights workers vanished in Philadelphia, Mississippi, many accused the local police of a racist murder. The trio had not been seen after being arrested on a speeding charge. The British *Daily Telegraph* reported;

The local sherriff had a Ku Klux Klan recruiting poster prominently displayed on the public notice board outside his office . . . open talk in the area is that the Klan "knows but ain't saying nuthin' ". . . . There is even speculation that they were beaten up so severely while in police custody that one succumbed and all three had to be taken for the proverbial ride [i.e. were killed].

The Ku Klux Klan was a racist organization set up after the Civil War of 1861-5 to prevent Blacks gaining their rights by terrorizing them.

America's presidential elections

Lyndon Johnson, who had become US President on the death of Kennedy, was now obliged to stand for re-election. His opponent was the Republican, Senator Barry Goldwater. Most of those who felt the Democrats did too much for black people and not enough against Communists backed Goldwater. Goldwater was very right wing, calling for attacks on Communist countries, supporting Cuban exiles, and backing 'extremism'. This frightened off many moderate Republicans, who feared that if Goldwater became President he would start a nuclear war. Some right-wing Democrats backed Goldwater. Senator Thurlond said 'The Democrat Party . . . has repudiated the constitution of the US, it is leading the evolution of our nation to a socialist dictatorship' – but most agreed with a Goldwater advisor, William Seward, who resigned saying the Senator had been 'captured by a small group and pushed further to the right'. At the election in November, over 41 million voted for LBJ, and only 26 million for Goldwater.

General election in Britain

Party politics in Britain in 1964 were dominated by the general election, which everyone knew was coming. Labour had increased its support during 1963 and hoped to get a 100-seat majority in the House of Commons. The Tories recovered under Alec Douglas Home, however, and by August 1964 they had a slight lead in the opinion polls. Racism played a part in the election, Labour's Harold Wilson promising a race relations act if they came to power.

The election was fought partly on the state of the economy after what Labour called '13 wasted years' under the Tories. In February it was reported that Japan was making oil tankers for half a million pounds less each than Britain could, and this emphasized the problems British firms had selling goods abroad. In February, the balance of trade – the gap between what Britain bought from abroad and what it sold – was the worst ever, and Britain ended the year having bought £800 million worth of goods more than it sold. This was the main reason why Labour won the election on 15 October, but by a majority of only four seats (five including the speaker who did not vote) over all other parties combined.

British foreign policy

The major problem facing British governments abroad in 1964 was Southern Rhodesia. The white minority wanted independence for the country, but not democracy. Britain would allow independence only if the country was run by the majority.

British domestic policy

HAROLD WILSON BECAME PRIME MINISTER. He planned to tackle the economy with an incomes policy to hold down wages and on 9 December the TUC agreed to work with the government and employers on this issue. Law and order also made the headlines. Rioting between mods and rockers took place in Clacton at Easter, at Brighton and Margate at Whitsun, and in Hastings during August. A detective sergeant, Harold Challenor, was charged with having planted evidence on suspects in March and found to be insane. Three other policemen were sent to prison for helping him. On 21 December the House of Commons abolished hanging for murder. On 17 April the Great Train Robbers were found guilty and given heavy sentences. Seven got 30 years. But one of the robbers, Charles Wilson, managed to escape from prison on 12 August.

Harold Wilson, cultivating an image as a calm, wise politician.

Sino-Soviet relations deteriorate

THE ARGUMENT BETWEEN RUSSIA AND CHINA became more heated in 1964. In January, China decided to encourage supporters in foreign Communist parties against the Russians. In March the Chinese criticized Russia at the Afro-Asian Solidarity Council. In October the Chinese exploded their first atom bomb. Although Kruschev was forced to resign as Soviet leader in October – he was 70 years old – it was clear that the row between China and Russia would go on. Indeed, many capitalists thought China was now more of a danger than Russia. Leonid Brezhnev replaced Kruschev as Soviet premier.

Leonid Brezhnev at his desk in the Kremlin.

Liston v. Clay

THE BIGGEST SPORTING STORY of the year was the world heavyweight championship between Sonny Liston and Cassius Clay. Liston was a great champion, as he had proved by his fights with Floyd Patterson. Clay was extraordinary, nicknamed 'The Louisville Lip' because of his boasting and bragging. At the weigh-in before the fight, Clay was fined $2500 (£900) for screaming and shouting. A doctor said, 'Clay is emotionally unbalanced. He acts like a man in mortal fear of death'. Liston started the fight 7-1 favourite, but he caused a sensation when he was cut in the third round, took a beating from Clay and refused to come out for round seven. He said he had damaged his shoulder, but people were suspicious. Clay had signed a contract before the fight allowing Liston to promote Clay's next fight if Clay became world champion. Had Liston deliberately retired in order to promote Clay's next contest? The American Senate investigated but could not prove fraud.

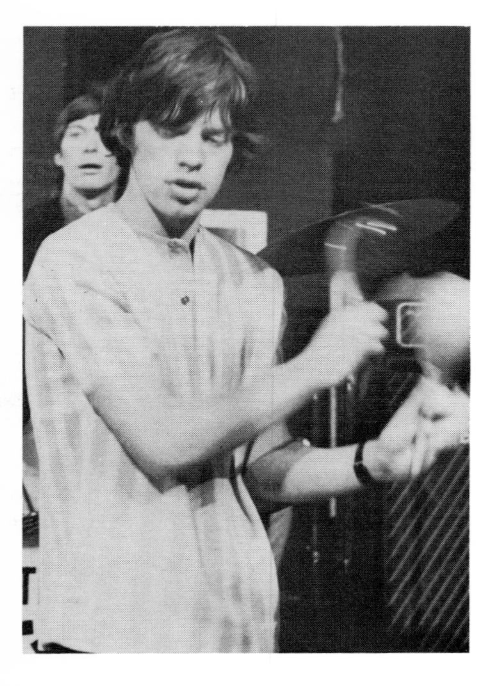

Mick Jagger leading the Rolling Stones on ITV's 'Ready Steady, Go!' in 1964.

'Pirate' radio

DISCONTENT AT THE LACK of pop music on BBC Radio led to the launch of several 'pirate' radio stations in 1964. On 28 March, Radio Caroline started from a boat moored five miles off Felixstowe. On 12 May Radio Atlanta began broadcasting from the boat *Mi Amigo* off the Essex/Suffolk coast, and soon 'pirate' boats were moored all round Britain.

Radio Sutch, organized and run by Mr David Sutch [Screaming Lord Sutch, the pop singer who unsuccessfully contested the Stratford by-election as an independent in August 1963] was installed in a disused gun tower on Shivering Sands, about four miles off Shoeburyness, Essex. It carried no advertisements, but Mr Sutch said that he hoped that little-known musical groups whose recordings the station broadcast might contribute to its costs if they subsequently became famous.

Popular music

MEANWHILE IN 1964, pop music lost its tacky, show-biz image. In April the American folk trio Peter, Paul and Mary played London for the first time, followed the same month by the folk superstar, Bob Dylan. Dylan's song 'Blowing in the Wind' became a hit both sides of the Atlantic. The Beatles followed up their 1963 success in Europe by storming America. At one point they had the top five positions in the American Top Ten. They made their first film, *A Hard Day's Night*. A psychologist said 'Very young girls see the Beatles as cuddlesome pets', and likened Beatlemania to the frenzied dancing and shouting of voodoo worshippers. Many young people wanted a more 'macho' group than the Beatles and were turning to the Rolling Stones. The Stones, who had their first Number 1 in 1964, became the focus of the teenage rebellion.

The Stones represent . . . an easy way to enrage parents. . . . They would flaunt their contempt, their sexuality, their inability to suffer fools gladly without any concession either in public or private. Even when they accepted a traditional show-biz chore, 'Sunday Night at the London Palladium', for example . . . they wouldn't give an inch. . . . Whatever happened to the Stones – they were fined for pissing against the wall of a garage, they were constantly being thrown out of hotels – was good news . . . the more they were hated by people over 30 the more they would be loved by every resentful teenager.
G. Melly, *Revolt into Style.*

Theatre and films

THE FLOW OF FINE PLAYS and films continued. Harold Pinter scored another success with the screenplay to his play *The Caretaker*. Directed by Clive Donner, it had three excellent actors in Alan Bates, Donald Pleasance and Robert Shaw. Richard Burton, seen in 1963 in *Cleopatra*, starred this year with Peter O'Toole in the film of Jean Anouilh's *Becket*. Later he would rejoin Elizabeth Taylor in a film of another 1964 stage hit, Edward Albee's *Who's Afraid of Virginia Woolf?*

Experimental drama flourished in 1964. In January the Royal Shakespeare Theatre announced a Theatre of Cruelty season, and in August, Peter Brook directed a production of Peter Weiss's play on the murder of the French revolutionary Jean Paul Marat, known as the *Marat/Sade*. This was set in the time of the French Revolution and the action took place in a madhouse. It was the most famous of the Theatre of Cruelty school of drama.

A different kind of artistic experiment was Arnold Wesker's Centre 42, which stopped travelling the country and launched an appeal in July to convert a building in London for a permanent base.

China gets the A-bomb

In 1964, China joined the USA, Russia, Britain and France as a country with the atom bomb. She exploded her first atom bomb on 16 October, and, while she did not have bombers or rockets powerful enough to attack the major powers, it was an important development. In April, captured documents showed that the Chinese did not fear the atom bomb because they thought they could survive even the terrible loss of life of a nuclear war as their population was so huge. They did promise, however, not to be the first to use the bomb.

China exploded an atom bomb at 1500 hours on October 16th, 1964, and thereby conducted successfully its first nuclear test. This is a major achievement of the Chinese people in their struggle to increase their national defence capability and oppose the US imperialist policy of nuclear blackmail and nuclear threats.

. . . The Chinese government has consistently advocated the complete prohibition and thorough destruction of nuclear weapons. But this position of ours has met the stubborn resistance of the US Imperialists. The Chinese government pointed out that the treaty on the partial halting of nuclear tests signed by the United States, Britain, and the Soviet Union in Moscow in July 1963 was a big fraud to fool the people of the world; that it tried to consolidate the nuclear monopoly held by the three nuclear powers and tie the hands and feet of the peace-loving countries. . .

The Chinese government hereby solemnly declares that China will never at any time and under any circumstances be the first to use nuclear weapons. . .

Hsinhua News Agency, Peking, 16 October 1964

Progress in space

On 3 February an American moon probe – Ranger 6 – hit the moon and was destroyed. The Americans still hailed this as a success, as their previous 11 missions had been lost in space. Unfortunately, the cameras did not work, and so no photographs were sent back. On 9 April the Americans sent up the first Gemini space capsule on a Titan rocket. The Gemini was a two-person satellite which could spend up to a fortnight in space, and was a major step towards sending men to the moon. The one person satellites the Americans had sent round the earth were not big enough to go to the moon. On 28 July, America launched the moon probe Ranger 7, and this time, on 1 August, its six cameras worked and sent back 4000 photographs in 15 minutes. Though it hit the Sea of Clouds at 5850 m.p.h and was destroyed it had done all the Americans had wanted. Lyndon Johnson congratulated the scientists on 'a tremendous technical achievement'.

The ominous mushroom cloud of China's first A-bomb explosion.

The search for speed

Concorde continued to attract attention. At the end of January, British Overseas Airways and Air France both ordered the plane, though the first one had yet to be built. Everyone seemed to want to travel faster. On 17 July the land speed record was broken by Donald Campbell. On Lake Eyrie in America he drove his car, Bluebird, at 403 m.p.h. The growth of interest in cars and aeroplanes meant an increasing demand for oil, and on 18 September the British government granted licences to oil companies to drill in the North Sea.

Dr Leakey's discovery

On 20 March the Tanganyikan government announced the discovery of a new species of early man, called *Homo Habilis* in the African Olduvai Gorge. The discovery was made by Dr Louis Leakey, the British anthropologist who in 1959 had unearthed the skull of another ancient form of man, called *Zinjanthropus*. The statement indicated that the finds of 1959 and 1964 showed that two distinct types of hominids (human beings) had been evolving in East Africa nearly two million years ago.

'The new species of the genus homo [man] is represented by the remains of five individuals; their type indicates a true member of homo with a very small brain, but closely resembling man as we know him to day. It seems probable that the species was ancestral to modern races of man. The discovery of the new species is of the greatest scientific importance, since it indicates that the common idea that there were three successive stages of homonid . . . is invalid, and that at least two separate branches were evolving contemporarily'.

Statement of the Tanganyika government, 20 March, 1964

1965

Violence against civil rights

DESPITE THE 1964 Civil Rights Bill, American blacks still found themselves having to struggle for their rights and facing violence when they did so. On 19 January, Martin Luther King was attacked by a white man in Selma, Alabama, a town now the centre of the voter campaign. In February a court ordered that the literacy test in Selma – said to test whether voters could read and write, but really designed to stop blacks voting – should be illegal. This sparked further white violence. On 8 March the Selma police attacked a peaceful black march with clubs, bull whips and ropes. Sixty-seven people were injured, and John Lewis, Chair of the Student Non-violent Co-ordinating Committee, ended up in hospital with a suspected fractured skull. On 10 March a white clergyman was beaten by five other whites after leaving a black church. He also had a fractured skull.

The law was little use in protecting civil rights workers against attack. In March four whites were arrested after the racist Ku Klux Klan killed a white woman helping blacks. Racist juries in the South would not convict. In October a white racist who admitted killing a Roman Catholic priest but said he had been attacked with a gun, was acquitted. No gun was produced. Later in the month it was revealed that 27 civil rights workers had been killed over the past five years, but no one had been convicted.

Smoke rises from burning buildings in Los Angeles' Watts ghetto during the uprising.

to anger

Blacks right to vote

PRESIDENT JOHNSON PROPOSED more laws to help blacks. On 16 March he went to Congress to ask for an extension of government power to help blacks get the right to vote. He sang the civil rights song 'We Shall Overcome'. The following are extracts from his speech to Congress:

This was the first nation in the history of the world to be founded with a purpose. The great phrases of that purpose still sound in every American heart, North and South – 'All men are created equal' – 'Government by the consent of the governed' – 'Give me liberty or give me death'. . . .

Those words are a promise to every citizen that he shall share in the dignity of man. This dignity cannot be found in a man's possessions, or his power, or his position. It rests on his right to be treated as a man equal in opportunity to all others. . . .

To apply any other test – to deny a man his hopes because of his race or colour, his religion or the place of his birth – is not only to do injustice, it is to deny America. . . .

The Constitution says no person shall be kept from voting because of his race or colour. We have all sworn an oath before God to support and defend that constitution. We must now act in obedience to that oath. . . .

We Shall Overcome

**We shall overcome,
We shall overcome,
We shall overcome, Some day,
O Deep in my heart, I do believe,
That we shall overcome Some Day.**

**We'll walk hand in hand,
We'll walk hand in hand,
We'll walk hand in hand, Some Day,
O Deep in my heart, I do believe,
That we'll walk hand in hand, Some Day.**

**We shall all be free,
We shall all be free,
We shall all be free, Some Day,
O Deep in my heart, I do believe,
That we shall all be free, Some Day.**

**We shall end Jim Crow,
We shall end Jim Crow,
We shall end Jim Crow, Some Day,
O Deep in my heart, I do believe,
That we shall end Jim Crow, Some Day,**

A beautiful old American folk song whose verses could be changed to suit many occasions. 'Jim Crow' means racial prejudice in the American South.

The Watts riots

ON 26 MAY THE SENATE PASSED a bill guaranteeing the blacks' right to vote. But many blacks had lost patience with laws and non-violent protest. In August the worst black demonstration yet took place, when the Watts area of Los Angeles exploded in three days of rioting. Twenty-eight people were killed, 1000 fires were reported, and it took 18,000 armed National Guards to stop the violence. Once again, President Johnson spoke out:

The riots in Los Angeles are more than a State concern. It is not simply that what has happened there can happen elsewhere. It is also that the Los Angeles disorders flow from a violent breach of rooted American principles.

The first is that injustices of our society shall be overcome by the peaceful processes of our society. There is no greater wrong in our democracy than violent, wilful disregard of law. . .

But it is not enough simply to decry disorder. We must also strike at the conditions from which disorder largely flows. For the second great American principle is that all shall have an equal chance to share in the blessings of our society. . .

We must not let anger drown understanding if domestic peace is ever to rest on its sure foundation – the faith of all our people that they share, in opportunity and obligation, the promise of American life. . .

Vietnam blues

EVEN MORE SERIOUS were the growing protests against the war in Vietnam. Unlike the Korean War of the early 1950s, American opinion was divided on Vietnam. Many Vietnamese also opposed the US involvement, and in February a Buddhist burnt herself to death in protest against America intervention.

On 19 April, 15,000 people demonstrated outside the President's home, the White House in Washington, against the American bombing of North Vietnam. As the USA sent more and more troops to Vietnam, young civilians were 'drafted' into the army to fight. Many Americans opposed being called up and took to burning their draft cards in public to show they would not go. In October the government called up 45,000 young men into the army, and on the 17th, 10,000 people demonstrated in New York and 4000 in California. 150,000 people were involved in the campaign against the draft, and a booklet was printed telling young men how to avoid it. On 18 October the first Vietnam protestor was arrested – a Roman Catholic pacifist. The war was becoming the biggest issue in American life.

Hanoi's children learn to watch for US planes and hide from bombs.

Vietnam crisis deepens

DURING 1965 THE VIETNAM WAR intensified. The USA put more and more effort into it, and the South Vietnamese government's lack of control became apparent. In August it was estimated that the Vietcong controlled a quarter of the country, the government about half, and the rest was not controlled by anyone. In the Vietcong areas the Communists had taken land from the few rich landowners and given it to the many poor peasants. This obviously made them more popular with the peasants. The South Vietnamese army was now too weak to fight the Communists, and the US decided she would take over the fighting leaving the Vietnamese simply to defend the land they controlled.

The war grew worse. By April the US was bombing North Vietnam every day. The Russians sent anti-aircraft missiles to help the Communists defend themselves from air attack. North Vietnam was friendly with the Chinese Communists, and the USA feared the Chinese would help the North Vietnamese, perhaps by launching an air attack in Korea to divert the US army. In June, America warned that she would use nuclear weapons against China if this happened. The real problem for the US was within Vietnam, however. By the end of June the Vietcong had camps seven miles from the South Vietnamese capital, Saigon. America prepared to throw more forces into the war, and a new word came into the language – 'escalation', meaning stepping up the effort.

Rhodesia breaks away

BRITAIN FACED HER OWN REBELLION in a distant land, Southern Rhodesia. Negotiations over independence continued, with the white minority refusing to give up power. In April, Prime Minister Ian Smith called an election, asking the whites-only voters to opt for independence without British consent. Over two-thirds did so. British Prime Minister, Harold Wilson, and other British ministers went to Salisbury, Rhodesia's capital, but Ian Smith refused to accept the five British principles on which independence depended, and on 11 November Ian Smith declared UDI – a Unilateral Declaration of Independence. On 16 November, Britain passed a sanctions bill, stopping trade with Rhodesia, on 17 December the British banned oil shipments, and on 27 December, Ian Smith introduced petrol rationing.

Southern Rhodesian Prime Minister, Ian Smith, the champion of independence for Rhodesia, calles for support at the general election.

Communist splits continue

IN 1965, THE RUSSIAN PREMIER Kosygin, went to see Mao Zedong, but this did not heal the splits between the Communists. When Russia called a conference of Communist countries, China and four allies – North Korea, North Vietnam, Indonesia and Rumania – refused to go. But China's allies in Indonesia had a major defeat when a Communist takeover was crushed in October. In Cuba, however, another of China's friends, Che Guevara, decided to leave the government and fight for revolution in South America.

Domestic affairs in Britain

Major reforms of 1965
- * Race relations board set up.
- * Abolition of hanging confirmed.
- * Policy of turning secondary schools comprehensive adopted.
- * Britain to abandon imperial measurements and to adopt metric system.

THE MAJOR PROBLEM FACING Labour's new government in 1965 was the poor state of the economy. The government decided the main cause was that Britain was awarding herself pay rises she had not earned. In March a new Prices and Incomes Board was set up, with Aubrey Jones, a Tory MP, as its chair. The government decreed that no one should get a pay increase of more than 3 per cent without the board's permission.

Labour's majority in the House of Commons was so small, however, that they had problems in getting enough votes. On 11 May Labour had a majority of only four when they tried to pass a bill nationalizing the steel industry, one MP coming from hospital to vote and another being brought by ambulance but being too ill to enter the building. On 26 May, Labour had only a one-vote majority and on 2 June there was a dead heat – 281 to 281 – because five Labour MPs were late for the vote. In September the Labour Party came to an arrangement with the Liberals, who agreed to give them their support so long as Labour was not socialist. In November, Labour agreed, abandoning plans to nationalize steel for the time being.

Labour remained quite popular in the opinion polls, however, and the Tories decided to change their leader for the next election. Alec Douglas Home resigned and Edward Heath was elected.

There were few sensations this year, but on 9 June, Ronnie Biggs, leader of the Great Train Robbers, hit the headlines when he escaped from gaol and fled the country.

Peaceful protest

WITH THE DEFEAT of the Conservatives in October 1964, anti-nuclear protest in Britain seemed to be dying down. *The Times* reporter wrote of the 1965 CND demonstration:

After seven years of Easter marches, the demonstrators may look younger than ever, but if quietness, discipline and good humour are evidence of political maturity, then the Campaign for Nuclear Disarmament can look forward to nothing more than a placid old age as part of the British way of life.

1965 Sport and the Arts

Theatre

IN 1965 THE OUTPUT of good plays dried up, and many people thought that the period of exciting new talent was coming to an end. On 6 January George Devine, director of the English Stage Company, resigned after nine years. He said he was 'deeply tired' after producing 145 plays in those nine years. While he had been in charge, his company at the Royal Court Theatre had produced some of the best new plays, including John Osborne's first, very important, play, *Look Back in Anger*, in 1956. Devine's retirement marked the end of an era.

Sport

IN HORSE RACING, ARKLE crowned his remarkable career by winning the Gallagher and Hennessey Gold Cups, and in boxing Cassius Clay retained the world heavyweight championship by beating Sonny Liston in May and Floyd Patterson in November. The fight was stopped in the twelfth round and Clay was criticized for not knocking Patterson out, even though Patterson had a back injury. Many people did not think Clay a great champion, and *The Times* described him as 'a showman and a clever fighter without a punch'.

Folk protest

FOR POP FANS, 1965 was the year of 'folk protest'. Folk music made a breakthrough into the charts, especially the album charts. Bob Dylan, who influenced several songs on the Beatles 'Revolver' album, had hits with the albums 'Freewheelin', 'Times They Are A' Changin', and 'Bringing It All Back Home', Joan Baez took traditional folk songs into the charts, and the Byrds made folk rock Top Ten material. Folk pushed all but the best pop and top film albums into the shade in August.

Cinema

FILMS WERE MORE INTERESTING. In January, a classic musical, *My Fair Lady*, opened in London. In April the Italian director Antonioni produced a comment on modern life in *The Red Desert*, and John Schlesinger also made a serious movie about modern life, *Darling*, starring 1960s cult figure Julie Christie. Less obvious as a social comment was the excellent Len Deighton spy thriller, *The Ipcress File*, but the best film of the year was the light-hearted pop movie about sex and love by Richard Lester, *The Knack (and how to get it)*. Sex and love were topical.

Two surprises

IN NOVEMBER KENNETH TYNAN, the theatre critic, caused a sensation by using a four-letter word on television. Equally sensational, the Queen awarded the Beatles the MBE in June. Many people complained, but Liverpool MP, Eric Heffer, congratulated the Beatles in a Commons motion:

Recognizing the great good and happiness that the Beatles have brought to millions throughout the world, and furthermore being the first entertainment group that has caught the American market . . . the House strongly appreciates the action of Her Majesty in awarding the Beatles the MBE.

British album chart, 21 August 1965

1	(1)	HELP The Beatles
2	(2)	THE SOUND OF MUSIC Soundtrack
3	(4)	MARY POPPINS Soundtrack
4	(3)	JOAN BAEZ 5 Joan Baez
5	(5)	BRINGING IT ALL BACK HOME Bob Dylan
6	(6)	THE SHADOWS The Shadows
7	(8)	ALMOST THERE Andy Williams
8	(7)	JOAN BAEZ IN CONCERT Joan Baez
9	(–)	JOAN BAEZ
10	(9)	BEATLES FOR SALE The Beatles

Joan Baez poses for a publicity picture.

The first space walk

IMPORTANT DEVELOPMENTS in manned space flight took place in 1965. On 18 March a Soviet cosmonaut, Alexei Leonov, became the first person to travel in space outside a spacecraft when he left the two-berth spaceship Sunrise for 20 minutes. During his space walk he was linked to the spaceship by a 15-foot (5 m) cable. Had the cable broken, Leonov would have been lost in space for ever. Leonov returned to earth, fit and well, on 19 March, calming fears about dangerous levels of radiation in space. He gave an interview about his experience:

I did not feel any fear, only a sense of the infinite expanses and depths of the universe. . . . Then , too, I constantly felt the presence of people on earth and of the ship's commander. I was astonished by everything I saw when I found myself in space. The earth below was flat and its curvature only noticeable on the horizon. Right ahead of me was a black sky, very black. The stars were bright, not twinkling. The sun was not radiant, just a smooth disc without a halo [which] seemed to be welded into the black, velvet background.

Cosmonaut Leonov makes his historic space walk.

The Gemini missions

LATER IN MARCH, the United States sent up Virgil Grissom in its Gemini mission. Mercury had been for one person – Gemini took two. Grissom had flown in Mercury, and became the first person to fly in space twice. The USA pressed ahead. In June, Gemini 4 stayed up longer than all seven previous American space flights put together. In August, Gemini 5 beat the Russian record of 119 hours in space to stay up nearly 191 hours. In October, Gemini 6 completed the first space rendezvous, docking with an Agena unstaffed rocket sent up earlier.

Space probes

UNSTAFFED SPACECRAFTS made several important flights. The United States sent Ranger probes to the moon, and the Russians sent Luna vehicles. Rangers 8 and 9 sent back pictures before crashing, but several attempts by the Russians to land Luna probes softly on the moon failed. In July the American Mariner 4 probe took pictures as it passed Mars. In August a Luna probe took pictures of the dark side of the moon.

Space shots were carefully planned – a space probe had to chase its target as it orbited round the sun.

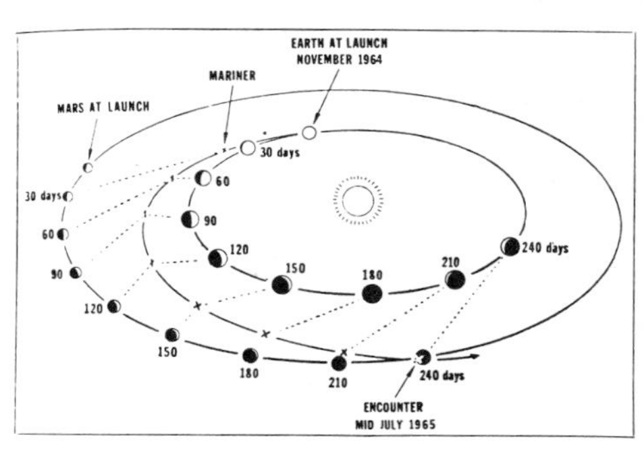

Telecommunications

MORE USEFUL THAN THE SPACE PROBES were telecommunication satellites. In April the USA sent up Early Bird, the world's first commercial communications satellite. It had 240 channels for transatlantic telephone and television relays, and weighed 85 lbs (39 kg). It was set to float 22,300 miles out in space. Back on earth, Harold Wilson opened the Post Office Tower in London, the hub of a network of microwave stations sending telephone messages without wires.

1966 China in

The bourgeois threat

DURING 1966, CHINA was swept by an enormous revolt, promoted by the Chinese Communist leader, Mao Zedong. The 'Cultural Revolution', as the revolt was called, grew from Chairman Mao's belief that true communism was being betrayed. This was part of the reason for the break with Russia which had startled the world in 1960.

Mao now believed, however, that communism was being threatened even inside China . He thought that the Chinese Communist Party had been taken over by 'bourgeois revisionists', people who were more interested in looking after their own interests than in the ideals of communism. Mao wanted to put China back on the road to pure communism – which he believed only he knew. In 1964 he had had a little red book of his ideas printed for the use of the army, *Quotations from Chairman Mao*. This book was to become world famous.

Mao and Lin Biao, visiting the Peking Opera, are saluted by an operatic version of 'Long Live Chairman Mao'.

Mao launches his campaign

MAO LAUNCHED HIS CAMPAIGN in late 1965. He did not have strong support in the capital, Beijing, because the Mayor opposed him. Nevertheless, control of the capital was vital if Mao was to take control of China, so he attacked the deputy Mayor, Wu Han. Amazingly, this started with an attack on a play that Wu Han had written in 1961. In September 1965, Mao criticized the play to top Chinese leaders. Mao could not get his criticisms published in Beijing, so sent his wife and secretary to Shanghai, where it was published in a local paper.

The mayor of Beijing, Peng Zhen, and his supporters defended Wu Han's play, and there was a bitter row. Mao now had the support of the leaders of the Communist Party, however, and on 30 April 1966 the Prime Minister, Zhou EnLai, announced the launching of the 'Cultural Revolution', calling for a struggle to wipe out 'bourgeois ideology [i.e. anti-Communist ideas] in . . . all . . . fields of culture'. In March, Mao had demanded Peng's sacking and arrest, and on 4 June Peng was finally dismissed.

Peng had been the sixth highest ranking Chinese official, and was only the third top Communist to be sacked since the revolution in 1949. On 7 June the editors of Beijing's three local papers were sacked, and there were demonstrations calling for the dismissal of Lu Ping, president of Beijing University. In July more leading Communists were sacked and professors at Beijing University were forced to wear placards saying 'I am an anti-Party intellectual'.

revolt

Propaganda team of Red Guards pose with Mao's Little Red Book.

Official Party policy

ON 8 AUGUST 1966 the Central Committee of the Chinese Communist Party published a document outlining the aims of the revolution:

Although the bourgeoisie has been overthrown, it is still trying to use the old ideas, culture, customs, and habits of the exploiting classes to corrupt the masses, capture their minds, and endeavour to stage a come-back. . . . Our objective is to struggle against and crush those persons in authority who are taking the capitalist road; to criticize and repudiate the reactionary bourgeois academic 'authorities' and the ideology of the bourgeoisie. . . .

Mao had not been seen for months, and rumours began to spread that he was dead. To disprove these, Mao swam in the Yangste river (he was 73) and his supporters claimed he had broken the Olympic record!

The revolution escalates

IN THE AUTUMN OF 1966 Red Guard activities spread all over China. On 4 November two million Red Guards demonstrated in Beijing, and on 16 November businessmen at the Canton Trade Fair had work interrupted for a lecture on the thoughts of Chairman Mao. On 23 November Red Guards in Beijing attacked Mao's main enemies, demanding the sacking of Liu Shaoqi, the Chairman of the People's Republic, and the Communist Party Secretary, Deng Xiaoping. On 23 November the workers at Beijing's biggest machine tools factory closed the gates to keep out Red Guards, and in a 15-hour battle 60 people were killed. The largest country in the world was, it seemed, falling apart.

The Red Guards

MAO FELT THAT IT WAS IMPORTANT that young people should understand the aims of communism, and he called upon students in schools and colleges to form Red Guard units to 'root out those who have taken the capitalist road'. On 29 August Red Guards demonstrated outside the Soviet Embassy and East German diplomats were attacked. The outside world could hardly understand why Communists were attacking Communists.

Red Guard units began carrying out search raids on people suspected of being anti-Communist, and a reign of terror began. One school pupil remembers an attack on one of his teachers:

Teacher Yang, advanced in age and suffering from high blood pressure, was dragged out at 11.30, and exposed to the summer sun for more than two hours . . . he was dragged up to the fourth floor of a building and down again, being savagely beaten. Imagine, a man over 60 years of age! He passed out several times, but was brought back to consciousness each time with cold water splashed on to his face. . .

This lasted for six hours, until he collapsed. They dragged him on to the athletics field and again poured cold water on him. Even the killers were stunned momentarily for this was probably the first time they had ever beaten a man to death.

Quoted in *The Times*, 6 January 1970

Vietnam

Vietnam was the most important world story in 1966, as the war grew worse. The United States continued her policy of sending troops into South Vietnam while using her air force to bomb both the Vietcong and the North Vietnamese. In January, America increased her army to over three million, with 200,000 soldiers in Vietnam. Trouble with the Buddhists increased, and in May and June the Saigon government had to send troops and tanks into Hue and Da Nang to capture the Buddhist pagodas and prevent Buddhist riots. On 1 July, Thich Nhat Hanh, director of the Institute of Social Studies at the Buddhist University of Saigon in Paris, put forward the Buddhist view of the war.

The Buddhists' action . . . represents the mobilization of the nationalist forces which do not form part of the Liberation Front against a government which appears simply as an extension of US foreign policy. . . .

The Buddhists do not accept the argument that there is no other choice than victory or surrender. Another possibility would be offered by a combination of the following initiatives; an end of bombing in the North and the South, an end of all offensive military action by the Americans, and the formation of an independent non-military government . . . a solemn engagement to withdraw the US troops at a specified date, after a limited period, might be made convincing by a US initiative on a significant scale. . . .

Of course, the North Vietnamese must also withdraw their troops. . . . But during my tour, I am not emphasizing that problem. . . . For many Westerners it is tempting to free themselves from a guilt complex about America's actions by claiming that Washington intervened because of a North Vietnamese invasion. There was not serious infiltration from the North before US domination of the South had become a reality and the Saigon government had refused to hold the promised elections.

In June, America decided to bomb Vietcong supply lines to stop supplies getting from North Vietnam to the National Liberation Front in the South. America's allies were not united on the war, however. Australia and South Korea sent troops but Britain refused to do so, and in September and October General de Gaulle called on the United States to withdraw, saying a military victory was impossible. He spoke from experience – the French had been defeated by Communists in Vietnam in 1954. At the end of December an American journalist, Harrison Salisbury, visited Hanoi and witnessed American bombing of civilian areas – something America claimed did not happen.

Buddhists in South Vietnam.

Shifting sands

The isolation of China was further increased in March, when Cuba broke off diplomatic links. Meanwhile, in Europe, France shook the NATO alliance when, in March, de Gaulle decided to take France out of the pact.

Violence dominates the US stage

Racial conflict continued, sadly, to dominate news from America. Blacks made some gains in 1966 – the first black to sit in the Cabinet was appointed, the first black nominated for a state legislature for nearly a hundred years took his place, and, in November, the first black senator was elected. The news was mostly bad, however. In March two people were killed in a further riot in Watts, the first of a series of race riots in 1966. Still worse, a peaceful march in Mississippi for civil rights hit trouble on 6 June when the black leader, James Meredith, was shot by a white racist. Martin Luther King took over the march, but when Meredith rejoined the march on 26 June after treatment the mood had changed. Meredith said; 'The first time I carried a Bible; next time I carry a gun'. Hopes of peaceful progress were dying. On 6 July the Congress of Racial Equality voted to take up the militant campaign for Black Power, and though Congress passed a third, stronger, Civil Rights Bill, Martin Luther King's hopes for non-violent advance seemed to be fading.

The French left troops in West Germany to protect the West Germans, but the Supreme Headquarters Allied Powers in Europe (SHAPE) had to move to Belgium. During the year, news began to arrive that a new tragedy was developing in Africa. In Nigeria, tribal conflict began in July when General Ironsi, head of the army, was killed by Hausa tribesmen. Ironsi belonged to the Ibo tribe. The leading Ibo soldier, Colonel Ojukwu, suggested splitting Nigeria into tribal areas. This was not done. In October, Ibos living in the Hausa north of Nigeria were murdered, and many were forced to flee south.

General election in Britain

AT THE START OF 1966 the future of the Labour government was the big issue facing Britain. Labour could not go on much longer with a tiny majority, having to rely on Liberal support. In January a by-election at Hull gave Labour an increased majority, and Harold Wilson decided to call a general election. This was fought at the end of March, and Labour ran its campaign under the slogan 'You Know Labour Government Works'. The electorate agreed, and Labour won with a majority of 98, scoring 363 seats against the Tories 252, with 12 Liberals and two others.

Sanctions against Rhodesia

IN DECEMBER HAROLD WILSON met Ian Smith on the cruiser *Tiger* for talks on Rhodesia, but no agreement was made. The UN voted mandatory (compulsory) sanctions on 16 December.

New government faces difficulties

ALMOST STRAIGHT AWAY, however, Labour ran into trouble. The economy was still weak, and on 9 May the government introduced a selective employment tax on selected 'non-essential' industries. In July it introduced a price freeze, and in October took compulsory powers to impose a wages and prices freeze. The TUC backed the first, the Labour conference the second, but relations with the unions turned sour. In November unemployment rose to 2.3%, the highest since 1963. The government seemed to have lost control, and on 18 November the TUC broke links with the government over the pay freeze, one member saying 'It's the government's policy, let them get on with it'.

Social reforms

TWO MAJOR SOCIAL REFORMS were carried forward in 1966. In July, Liberal David Steele's abortion bill was introduced, and on 20 December male homosexuality was finally legalized. Following the showing of the programme 'Cathy Come Home' on television in November, the pressure group Shelter was set up to campaign for better housing.

In December the government decided that Britain should get rid of the old currency and go decimal.

The kind of housing conditions highlighted in Cathy Come Home *that led to the setting up of* Shelter.

Psychedelia

IN 1966 FRINGE ART – known as the 'Underground' – began to take the spotlight. In February a paperback edition of *The Lord of the Rings* was published. This was a huge story of elves and wizards by an Oxford don, J.R.R. Tolkien, which had sold 200,000 copies in the decade since it was published. It was to become a cult book among students. Meanwhile, drugs – especially LSD – were becoming increasingly popular as the Beatnik culture of California spread. In October the British *Melody Maker* magazine reported that 'psychedelic', meaning 'mind-expanding', was becoming the 'in' word. The advocates of mind-expanding drugs were led by Dr Timothy Leary, whose book *The Politics of Experience and the Bird of Paradise* said that only repressive governments stopped people entering a wonderful world of experience through drugs.

Psychedelia influenced pop through the so-called 'New Music', which was interested in the East and exotic religions, some of which used drugs. George Harrison led a craze for Eastern music – so-called 'Raga-rock' – and in June pop musician Steve Marriott commented 'We'll be able to get plastic sitars in our cornflakes soon', but vaguely drug-influenced music was more influential. In September, British folk singer Donovan topped the American charts with 'Sunshine Superman', and the Californian band The Beach Boys produced the first 'psychedelic' Number 1 in December with 'Good Vibrations'. Meanwhile, Bob Dylan, unelected leader of the 'New Music', suffered a serious motor bike accident in August which put him out of action for a year. In his absence, his followers elevated him to a semi God-like status, in which even his most trivial actions became almost mystical. Blues singer Tony Glover describes how to open Dylan's 'Blonde on Blonde' double album:

Opening it up even turns you around. You come and you take off that cellophane and you don't know how to open it. You can't just take it as another record because immediately it's in a different class. You gotta take it apart this way and which way is up and how do you get the records out and it's not something you can do automatically. You have to think about it.

Bobby Moore, English skipper, lifts the World Cup.

Clay joins Black Muslims

1966 WAS THE YEAR that Cassius Clay became accepted as a great world champion boxer and joined the Black Muslims. Clay, an intelligent black American, became disgusted with the treatment of blacks in the USA, and joined the Black Muslim church. He abandoned what he called his 'white' name and became Muhammad Ali. He fought well that year, beating Britain's Henry Cooper in May, and taking the World Boxing Association title off Ernie Terrell with what one writer called 'dazzling speed and punching power'.

England wins the World Cup

THE BIGGEST SPORTING STORY of 1966 in Britain was the World Cup. For the first time the world's biggest football championship was being held in Britain. England reached the semi-finals, where they met Portugal. Portugal had caused a sensation by knocking out the favourites, Brazil. Beating Portugal 2–1, England faced West Germany in a memorable final at Wembley. England were leading 2–1, but conceded an equalizer in the last minute of normal time. Then, in extra time, Geoff Hurst scored a controversial goal which bounced off the cross-bar on to the line and was ruled to have gone over. Hurst scored a second goal in the last period of extra time to make his own personal hat-trick and give England a 4–2 victory.

Astronauts Armstrong and Scott prepare to board the Gemini spacecraft.

Progress in space

THE US SPACE PROGRAMME proceeded well, despite near disaster. On 15 March, Gemini 8 successfully docked for the first time with an Agena target vehicle, making a historic link-up in space. On the return journey,

A short circuit in the manoeuvring control system on Gemini 8 had caused the spacecraft to tumble violently. . . Almost immediately the spacecraft began to tumble excessively, primarily in roll. The roll rates approached one revolution per second, and the crew realized they were approaching their physiological limits. In spite of this they were able to reactivate the spacecraft's manoeuvring system and activate the re-entry control system, with which they judiciously and slowly regained control. . .
NASA statement on the achievement of pilot Neil Armstrong and co-pilot Major David Scott.

On 6 June, Eugene Cernan spent two hours in space on the Gemini 9 mission. Six weeks later, Gemini 10 docked with an Agena vehicle and the two crafts went up 474 miles – a record height. Gemini 11 then set a new altitude record for piloted spacecraft of 853 miles. Gemini 12, which was the last Gemini mission, linked up with an Agena craft 180 miles over East Africa and went through 58 orbits in four days. The USSR continued with its moon programme and on 4 February, Luna 9 made the first soft landing on the moon. On 8 December the USA and USSR signed a treaty banning weapons from space.

Cables threatened

BACK ON EARTH, on 9 July it was revealed that the use of satellites for telephone messages was threatening the future of cable-laying ships. Cables had been the main way of sending telegraph and telephone messages for a century, but satellites were now as cheap as laying cables.

Dangers of atomic weapons

THE DANGER OF ATOMIC WEAPONS was emphasized when, on 7 January, a US aircraft dropped an atom bomb into the sea off the Spanish port of Palomares. It took the Americans two months to find the bomb, which they did on 21 March. However, it was perched on an underwater ledge, and before they could get it back it rolled off the ledge on 20 April, sinking deeper into the mud. On 7 May it was found 2500 feet under the water and was recovered.

1967 Peace, love

The 'Summer of Love'

1967 IS PROBABLY BEST REMEMBERED as the year of the 'Summer of Love', the summer when the hippies first became widely seen and reported. The hippies believed they had discovered a new, better way of living, which was peaceful and loving. They felt that people were being 'screwed up' by working all the time to buy things they didn't need, and that ruining their lives in this way led to violence. A better way of living was to explore the mind with drugs and 'drop out' of conventional society. Many followed exotic Eastern religions like Zen Buddhism or transcendental meditation.

Pilgrimage to San Francisco

MANY YOUNG AMERICANS, rejecting their parents' lifestyle (but often still living on their parents' money) went to California, and, in particular, to the town of San Francisco. Across the bay in the poor town of Oakland, some of the worst uprisings of black people took place, but San Francisco was rich and peaceful. As the summer developed, thousands of young people poured into the city. By July there were over 100,000 hippies, partly led there by Scott MacKenzie's Number 1 hit song 'If You're Going to San Francisco (Wear some Flowers in Your Hair)'. The hippies, it was said, believed that you could calm down violent people by giving them flowers.

The Beatles celebrate the release of 'Sergeant Pepper', John Lennon in full hippie gear.

The Human-be-in

EVENTS IN SAN FRANCISCO were broadcast to the world as they happened. A 'human-be-in', involving 300,000 people, seemed to show that large numbers of peaceful people could gather to hear music and poetry. Emmett Grogan, leader of an anarchist group in San Francisco., put forward a rather more cynical view.

The human-be-in was publicised as a 'Gathering of the Tribes', but it was actually more a gathering of the suburbs with only a sprinkling of non-whites. . . . It was a showcase for beaded hipsterism with only one stage for the Assembly to face . . . the Quicksilver Messenger Service, the (Jefferson) Airplane [Later Starship] and the Grateful Dead played their sets over a PA system guarded by Hells Angels who were asked to do so after several incidents had occured. . . .

More ham chewers trouped up to the mike and kept saying how wonderful it was with all that energy in one place at the same time. Just being. Being together, touching, looking, embracing each other – that's what it was all about, they said, 'The New Consciousness'! Then the mantra [chant] began; 'We are one! We are one!' Three hundred thousand people shouted repeatedly that they were one. . . .

Someone parachuted out of a single engined plane into the middle of the meadow and several thousand people began swearing that they just saw a vision of God. . . . The HIP merchants were astounded by their triumph in promoting such a large market for their wares. They became the Western World's tastemakers overnight. . . .

Emmett Grogan, in his autobiography, *Ringolevio*, 1972

In July a similar free concert was held in Hyde Park, addressed by the American beat-poet-turned-hippie, Allen Ginsberg.

and reality

All you need is love . . .

NOT ALL THE IDEAS travelled one way, from America to Britain, however. Indeed, the interest of the Beatles and Rolling Stones in drugs, and what were called 'psychedelic' experiences, was enormously influential. The Beatles had become interested in Eastern religions and Indian music in 1966. Their music became more and more experimental, culminating in the release, in May 1967, of their album 'Sergeant Pepper's Lonely Hearts Club Band'. The final track, 'A Day in the Life', had the whole London Symphony Orchestra playing their instruments from the bottom to the top of the register at the same time. The BBC thought this was an attempt to recreate a trip on the drug LSD, and banned the track.

On 21 June, Paul McCartney was criticized by preacher Billy Graham for admitting he had taken LSD. On 24 July all the Beatles signed an advert in *The Times* newspaper calling for the legalization of the soft drug cannabis. But no action was taken against the Beatles for drug use.

At the end of August, Mick Jagger of the Rolling Stones joined the Beatles in a trip to Bangor, North Wales, for meditation with the Indian guru, the Maharishi Mahesh Yogi. On the 28 August the trip had to be cut short – the Beatles manager, and their real guru, Brian Epstein, had been found dead. It was a turning point in the Beatles' career. Despite the success of their summer Number 1, 'All You Need is Love', it was clear that love was not enough.

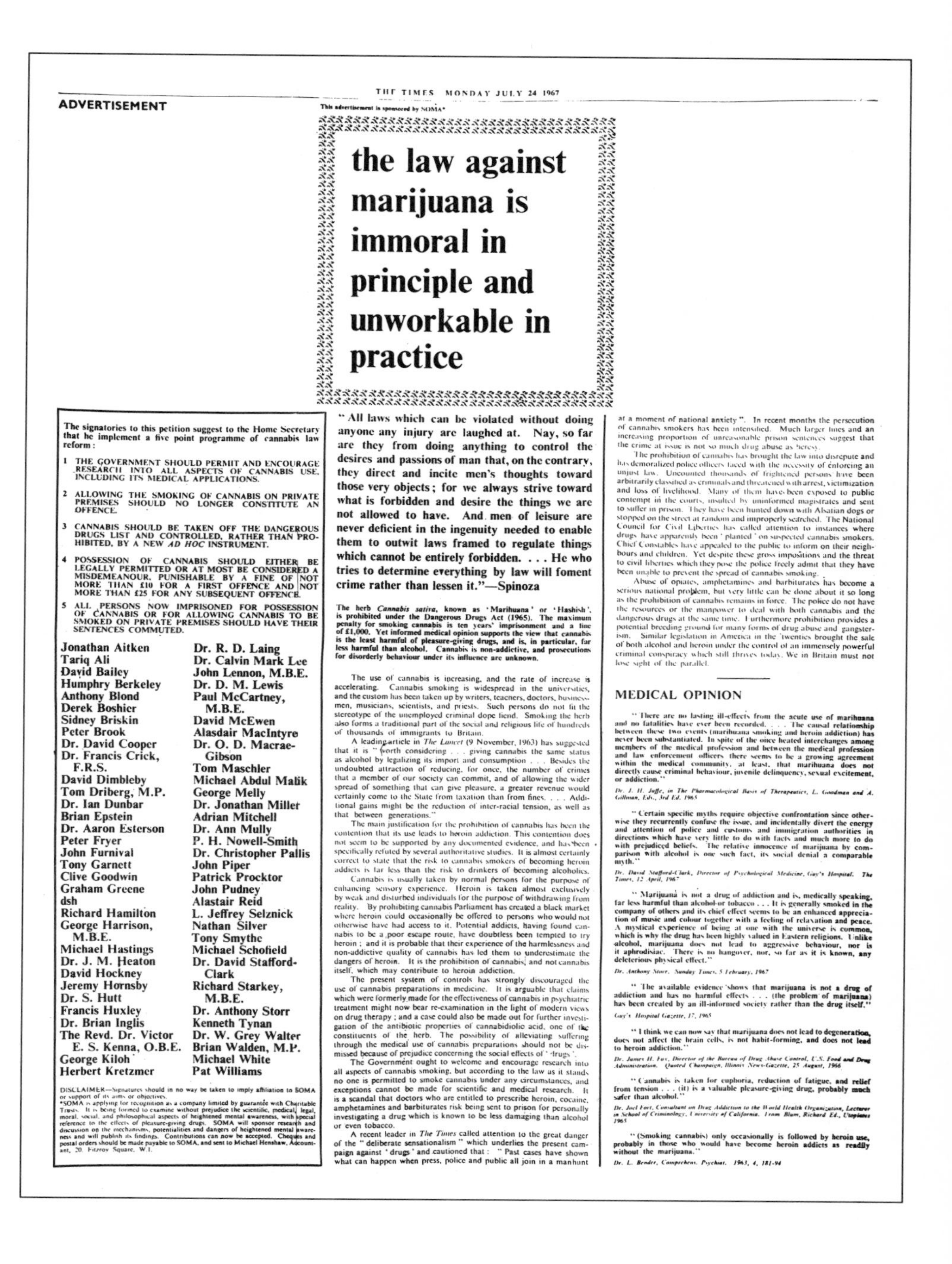

THE TIMES MONDAY JULY 24 1967

ADVERTISEMENT

This advertisement is sponsored by SOMA*

the law against marijuana is immoral in principle and unworkable in practice

The signatories to this petition suggest to the Home Secretary that he implement a five point programme of cannabis law reform:

1 THE GOVERNMENT SHOULD PERMIT AND ENCOURAGE RESEARCH INTO ALL ASPECTS OF CANNABIS USE, INCLUDING ITS MEDICAL APPLICATIONS.

2 ALLOWING THE SMOKING OF CANNABIS ON PRIVATE PREMISES SHOULD NO LONGER CONSTITUTE AN OFFENCE.

3 CANNABIS SHOULD BE TAKEN OFF THE DANGEROUS DRUGS LIST AND CONTROLLED, RATHER THAN PROHIBITED, BY A NEW *AD HOC* INSTRUMENT.

4 POSSESSION OF CANNABIS SHOULD EITHER BE LEGALLY PERMITTED OR AT MOST BE CONSIDERED A MISDEMEANOUR, PUNISHABLE BY A FINE OF NOT MORE THAN £10 FOR A FIRST OFFENCE AND NOT MORE THAN £25 FOR ANY SUBSEQUENT OFFENCE.

5 ALL PERSONS NOW IMPRISONED FOR POSSESSION OF CANNABIS OR FOR ALLOWING CANNABIS TO BE SMOKED ON PRIVATE PREMISES SHOULD HAVE THEIR SENTENCES COMMUTED.

Jonathan Aitken
Tariq Ali
David Bailey
Humphry Berkeley
Anthony Blond
Derek Boshier
Sidney Briskin
Peter Brook
Dr. David Cooper
Dr. Francis Crick, F.R.S.
David Dimbleby
Tom Driberg, M.P.
Dr. Ian Dunbar
Brian Epstein
Dr. Aaron Esterson
Peter Fryer
John Furnival
Tony Garnett
Clive Goodwin
Graham Greene
dsh
Richard Hamilton
George Harrison, M.B.E.
Michael Hastings
Dr. J. M. Heaton
David Hockney
Jeremy Hornsby
Dr. S. Hutt
Francis Huxley
Dr. Brian Inglis
The Revd. Dr. Victor E. S. Kenna, O.B.E.
George Kiloh
Herbert Kretzmer
Dr. R. D. Laing
Dr. Calvin Mark Lee
John Lennon, M.B.E.
Dr. D. M. Lewis
Paul McCartney, M.B.E.
David McEwen
Alasdair MacIntyre
Dr. O. D. Macrae-Gibson
Tom Maschler
Michael Abdul Malik
George Melly
Dr. Jonathan Miller
Adrian Mitchell
Dr. Ann Mully
P. H. Nowell-Smith
Dr. Christopher Pallis
John Piper
Patrick Procktor
John Pudney
Alastair Reid
L. Jeffrey Selznick
Nathan Silver
Tony Smythe
Michael Schofield
Dr. David Stafford-Clark
Richard Starkey, M.B.E.
Dr. Anthony Storr
Kenneth Tynan
Dr. W. Grey Walter
Brian Walden, M.P.
Michael White
Pat Williams

DISCLAIMER—Signatures should in no way be taken to imply affiliation to SOMA or support of its aims or objectives.

*SOMA is applying for recognition as a company limited by guarantee with Charitable Trusts. It is being formed to examine without prejudice the scientific, medical, legal, moral, social, and philosophical aspects of heightened mental awareness, with special reference to the effects of pleasure-giving drugs. SOMA will sponsor research and discussion on the mechanisms, potentialities and dangers of heightened mental awareness and will publish its findings. Contributions can now be accepted. Cheques and postal orders should be made payable to SOMA, and sent to Michael Henshaw, Accountant, 20, Fitzroy Square, W.1.

"All laws which can be violated without doing anyone any injury are laughed at. Nay, so far are they from doing anything to control the desires and passions of man that, on the contrary, they direct and incite men's thoughts toward those very objects; for we always strive toward what is forbidden and desire the things we are not allowed to have. And men of leisure are never deficient in the ingenuity needed to enable them to outwit laws framed to regulate things which cannot be entirely forbidden. . . . He who tries to determine everything by law will foment crime rather than lessen it."—Spinoza

The herb *Cannabis sativa*, known as 'Marihuana' or 'Hashish', is prohibited under the Dangerous Drugs Act (1965). The maximum penalty for smoking cannabis is ten years' imprisonment and a fine of £1,000. Yet informed medical opinion supports the view that cannabis is the least harmful of pleasure-giving drugs, and is, in particular, far less harmful than alcohol. Cannabis is non-addictive, and prosecutions for disorderly behaviour under its influence are unknown.

The use of cannabis is increasing, and the rate of increase is accelerating. Cannabis smoking is widespread in the universities, and the custom has been taken up by writers, teachers, doctors, businessmen, musicians, scientists, and priests. Such persons do not fit the stereotype of the unemployed criminal dope fiend. Smoking the herb also forms a traditional part of the social and religious life of hundreds of thousands of immigrants to Britain.

A leading article in *The Lancet* (9 November, 1963) has suggested that it is "worth considering . . . giving cannabis the same status as alcohol by legalizing its import and consumption . . . Besides the undoubted attraction of reducing, for once, the number of crimes that a member of our society can commit, and of allowing the wider spread of something that can give pleasure, a greater revenue would certainly come to the State from taxation than from fines. . . . Additional gains might be the reduction of inter-racial tension, as well as that between generations."

The main justification for the prohibition of cannabis has been the contention that its use leads to heroin addiction. This contention does not seem to be supported by any documented evidence, and has been specifically refuted by several authoritative studies. It is almost certainly correct to state that the risk to cannabis smokers of becoming heroin addicts is far less than the risk to drinkers of becoming alcoholics.

Cannabis is usually taken by normal persons for the purpose of enhancing sensory experience. Heroin is taken almost exclusively by weak and disturbed individuals for the purpose of withdrawing from reality. By prohibiting cannabis Parliament has created a black market where heroin could occasionally be offered to persons who would not otherwise have had access to it. Potential addicts, having found cannabis to be a poor escape route, have doubtless been tempted to try heroin; and it is probable that their experience of the harmlessness and non-addictive quality of cannabis has led them to underestimate the dangers of heroin. It is the prohibition of cannabis, and not cannabis itself, which may contribute to heroin addiction.

The present system of controls has strongly discouraged the use of cannabis preparations in medicine. It is arguable that claims which were formerly made for the effectiveness of cannabis in psychiatric treatment might now bear re-examination in the light of modern views on drug therapy; and a case could also be made out for further investigation of the antibiotic properties of cannabidiolic acid, one of the constituents of the herb. The possibility of alleviating suffering through the medical use of cannabis preparations should not be dismissed because of prejudice concerning the social effects of 'drugs'.

The Government ought to welcome and encourage research into all aspects of cannabis smoking, but according to the law as it stands no one is permitted to smoke cannabis under any circumstances, and exceptions cannot be made for scientific and medical research. It is a scandal that doctors who are entitled to prescribe heroin, cocaine, amphetamines and barbiturates risk being sent to prison for personally investigating a drug which is known to be less damaging than alcohol or even tobacco.

A recent leader in *The Times* called attention to the great danger of the "deliberate sensationalism" which underlies the present campaign against 'drugs' and cautioned that: "Past cases have shown what can happen when press, police and public all join in a manhunt at a moment of national anxiety". In recent months the persecution of cannabis smokers has been intensified. Much larger fines and an increasing proportion of unreasonable prison sentences suggest that the crime at issue is not so much drug abuse as heresy.

The prohibition of cannabis has brought the law into disrepute and has demoralized police officers faced with the necessity of enforcing an unjust law. Uncounted thousands of frightened persons have been arbitrarily classified as criminals and threatened with arrest, victimization and loss of livelihood. Many of them have been exposed to public contempt in the courts, insulted by uninformed magistrates and sent to suffer in prison. They have been hunted down with Alsatian dogs or stopped on the street at random and improperly searched. The National Council for Civil Liberties has called attention to instances where drugs have apparently been 'planted' on suspected cannabis smokers. Chief Constables have appealed to the public to inform on their neighbours and children. Yet despite these gross impositions and the threat to civil liberties which they pose the police freely admit that they have been unable to prevent the spread of cannabis smoking.

Abuse of opiates, amphetamines and barbiturates has become a serious national problem, but very little can be done about it so long as the prohibition of cannabis remains in force. The police do not have the resources or the manpower to deal with both cannabis and the dangerous drugs at the same time. Furthermore prohibition provides a potential breeding ground for many forms of drug abuse and gangsterism. Similar legislation in America in the 'twenties brought the sale of both alcohol and heroin under the control of an immensely powerful criminal conspiracy which still thrives today. We in Britain must not lose sight of the parallel.

MEDICAL OPINION

"There are no lasting ill-effects from the acute use of marihuana and no fatalities have ever been recorded. . . . The causal relationship between these two events (marihuana smoking and heroin addiction) has never been substantiated. In spite of the once heated interchanges among members of the medical profession and between the medical profession and law enforcement officers there seems to be a growing agreement within the medical community, at least, that marihuana does not directly cause criminal behaviour, juvenile delinquency, sexual excitement, or addiction."

Dr. J. H. Jaffe, in The Pharmacological Basis of Therapeutics, L. Goodman and A. Gillman, Eds., 3rd Ed. 1965

"Certain specific myths require objective confrontation since otherwise they recurrently confuse the issue, and incidentally divert the energy and attention of police and customs and immigration authorities in directions which have very little to do with facts and much more to do with prejudiced beliefs. The relative innocence of marijuana by comparison with alcohol is one such fact, its social denial a comparable myth."

Dr. David Stafford-Clark, Director of Psychological Medicine, Guy's Hospital. The Times, 12 April, 1967

"Marijuana is not a drug of addiction and is, medically speaking, far less harmful than alcohol or tobacco . . . It is generally smoked in the company of others and its chief effect seems to be an enhanced appreciation of music and colour together with a feeling of relaxation and peace. A mystical experience of being at one with the universe is common, which is why the drug has been highly valued in Eastern religions. Unlike alcohol, marijuana does not lead to aggressive behaviour, nor is it aphrodisiac. There is no hangover, nor, so far as it is known, any deleterious physical effect."

Dr. Anthony Storr. Sunday Times, 5 February, 1967

"The available evidence shows that marijuana is not a drug of addiction and has no harmful effects . . . (the problem of marijuana) has been created by an ill-informed society rather than the drug itself."

Guy's Hospital Gazette, 17, 1965

"I think we can now say that marijuana does not lead to degeneration, does not affect the brain cells, is not habit-forming, and does not lead to heroin addiction."

Dr. James H. Fox, Director of the Bureau of Drug Abuse Control, U.S. Food and Drug Administration. Quoted Champaign, Illinois News-Gazette, 25 August, 1966

"Cannabis is taken for euphoria, reduction of fatigue, and relief from tension . . . (it) is a valuable pleasure-giving drug, probably much safer than alcohol."

Dr. Joel Fort, Consultant on Drug Addiction to the World Health Organization, Lecturer in School of Criminology, University of California. From Blum, Richard Ed., Utopiates 1965

"(Smoking cannabis) only occasionally is followed by heroin use, probably in those who would have become heroin addicts as readily without the marijuana."

Dr. L. Bender, Comprehens. Psychiat. 1963, 4, 181-94

This advertisement for the legalization of cannabis was published in The Times *on 24 July 1967.*

US troops in Vietnam

Date	US troops	No. killed
1961	3,200	42
1962	11,300	42
1963	16,300	78
1964	23,300	147
1965	184,000	1369
1966	389,000	5008
1967	449,000	3625*

*to 20 May

From *The Times*, 26 May 1987

It was the summer of love only for white hippies. Black riots occurred all over the USA that summer.

Vietnam

IN 1967 THE FIGHTING in Vietnam grew worse. The US air force was suffering badly from anti-aircraft missiles. By 7 February it had lost 1815 aircraft. America still believed it was winning, however. On 2 March Robert MacNamara, Secretary of War, claimed Vietcong dead were up 40% to 50% in the previous three months. But on 12 May it was revealed that the South Vietnamese army was unable to protect villages from Vietcong attack. On 13 July, President Johnson authorized sending 100,000 more troops to Vietnam, bringing the total there to over half a million. On 20 September, the Chinese Nationalist Embassy in Saigon was blown up by the Vietcong, and the Commander-in-Chief of the US Pacific fleet called for the mining of North Vietnam's Haiphong harbour to stop supplies to North Vietnam. On 22 October a Buddhist nun burned herself to death, and on 1 November the US Vice President was shelled by Vietcong as he arrived in Saigon.

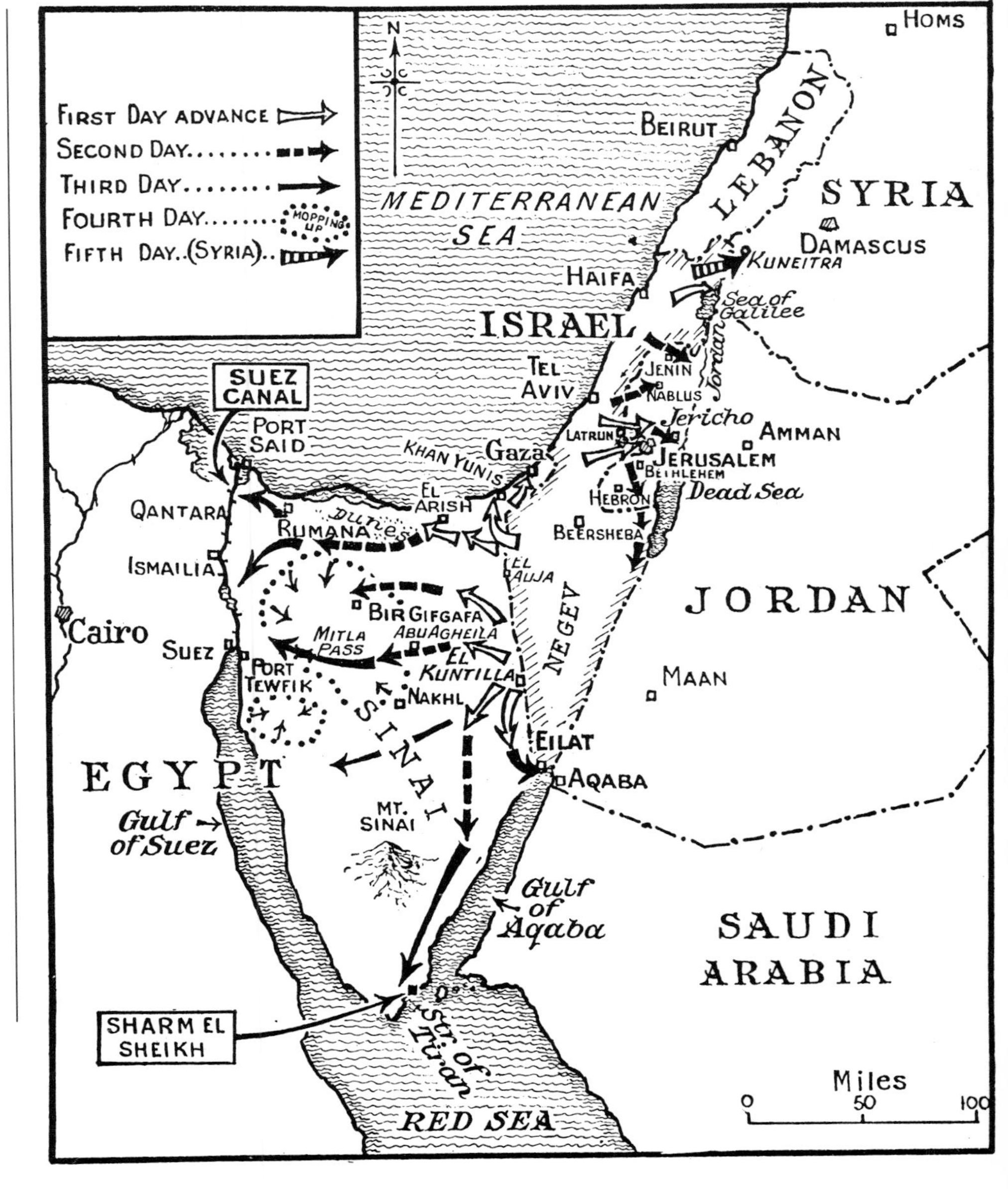

Map published in the Sunday Telegraph, *showing Israel's day-by-day advances during the Six-Day War.*

The USA

THE WAR IN VIETNAM increased trouble in America. Blacks pointed out that black soldiers in Vietnam suffered unfairly: 10% of the population of the United States was black, 12.5% of the American army was black, 14.6% of battle-dead was black. On 23 April, Muhammad Ali called the war a race war – 'Black men are being cut up by white men' – and on 28 April he refused the call-up for the US army. The World Boxing Association stripped him of his world title, and on 21 June he was found guilty of avoiding the draft. He was given a five-year jail sentence, and appealed. By 1 August so many black uprisings had taken place during the 'Long Hot Summer' that a map had to be produced to show where they had happened.

The Six-Day War in the Middle East

THE ARABS HAD NEVER ACCEPTED the State of Israel, which had been declared in 1948, and had fought the Israelis in 1948 and 1956. They had lost on both occasions. In 1967 a third war looked likely. Egypt's President Nasser closed the Straits of Tiran to Israeli ships, and signed a treaty with Israel's enemy, King Hussein of Jordan. Believing she would be attacked, Israel struck first. On 5 June Israeli planes attacked Egypt's airfields and smashed her air force. Israeli tanks swept into Sinai and the left bank of the Jordan River and beat Egyptian and Jordanian troops. On the last day of the Six-Day War, Israel attacked and captured the Golan Heights from Syria. The three most dangerous Arab nations on Israel's borders had been defeated.

Che Guevara's legacy

CHE GUEVARA'S DEATH made him a martyr and a cult figure for revolutionaries everywhere. In 1969 the following letter was published in *The Great Rebel*, by Luis J. Gonzalez and Gustavo A. Sanchez Solazar:

To my dear children, Hildita, Adeilita, Camilo, Celia, and Ernesto:

If you ever have to read this letter, it will be because I am no longer among you.

You will hardly remember me, and the youngest children will not remember me at all.

Your father has always been a man who acted in accordance with what he thought, and there is no denying that he has been faithful to his convictions.

Grow up like good revolutionaries. Study a lot so as to master the technique that allows man to master nature. Remember that the revolution is the important thing, and that each of us is worth nothing alone.

Above all make yourself capable of responding in your heart of hearts to any injustice committed against anyone in any part of the world. This is the most beautiful quality in a revolutionary.

Good-by forever, children; I still hope to see you again. A big kiss and a big hug from Papa

Britain

IN 1967 THE LABOUR GOVERNMENT ran into trouble with both the electors and its own MPs. Harold Wilson was annoying his own supporters by not being left wing enough and the voters for being unsuccessful. The main reason for Labour's unpopularity was the continuing economic crisis. On 16 November the government decided to devalue the pound. This meant that imported goods would cost more, and exported goods would cost less. The Prime Minister, announcing the decision on 19 November, said the government hoped that this would solve the problem of economic expansion leading to floods of cheap imported goods. This did not satisfy the radicals.

Two important social issues were raised in 1967: Lord Gardiner called for change in the divorce law so that divorce would be allowed on the grounds the marriage had broken up; and on 19 July an important liberalization of sexual law took place when abortion was made legal.

China

IT WAS VERY DIFFICULT to get news from China, but the Cultural Revolution continued. On 13 January a Cultural Revolution Committee was set up for the army, which up to now had not been directly involved. On 21 January Lin Biao, leader of the People's Liberation Army, was quoted as saying the country was involved in a civil war. In March a 'Three Way Alliance' of Red Guards, the Army and party officials was announced. On 31 March the *People's Daily* appealed to army officers to back Mao. On 8 August Beijing Radio reported attempts by anti-Mao forces to take over the air force.

Violence was spreading throughout China, with the army splitting into pro- and anti-Mao forces. On 3 September Zhou Enlai issued a directive banning violent demonstrations against foreigners, and Red Guards in Beijing were reprimanded for using force. On 25 September the Chinese launched a campaign to stop the violence, under the slogan 'Support the Army and Love the People'. Mao toured five provinces – the first time he had been outside Beijing since 1958. On 26 October he dismissed the extreme left of the Central Committee. He seemed to be worried that the attack on the Party he had launched was damaging China.

1967 # Sport and the Arts

Films

IN JANUARY *The Sound of Music* opened in Britain. It did not attract much interest at first, but was to become one of the most popular films of all time. The most successful film at the Oscar awards, however, was the film of Robert Bolt's play *A Man for all Seasons*, which won six Oscars. *Who's Afraid of Virginia Woolf?*, directed by Mike Nichols, won five. Clint Eastwood starred as the man with no name in *A Fistful of Dollars* in June, and an even more violent film, the gangster movie *Bonnie and Clyde*, opened in September. Many people thought these two films glorified violence. In the British cinema Joseph Losey scored a success with *Accident*, while Peter Watkins failed with *Privilege*, despite having pop star Paul Jones and top model Jean Shrimpton.

Pop music

POP MUSIC WAS NOW BECOMING noticed as an art form. On 31 March, *The Times* started a pop column, written by Miles Kington, and ran a major review of the Beatles' 'Sergeant Pepper' album when it came out, as did many of the music magazines of the time.

We now have a masterpiece. Like the Beatles themselves, Sergeant Pepper is both enigmatic and brilliant. . . . listening to it is like solving a delicious puzzle – you think as you tap your feet.

The Beatles are resurrected . . . as a spangled and marvellous marching band of the mind (complete with a songbag full of the philosophic, the psychedelic, the autobiographical, and the home made! . . .) The fusion of themes is remarkable. Life and death? Yes – and on many different levels. . .
Paul Nelson in *Sing Out!*, the leading American folk song magazine, October/November 1967

The increase in popularity of pop music and the presence of the pirate radio stations forced the BBC to start an all-pop radio channel, Radio One, which began in September with DJ Tony Blackburn playing 'Flowers in the Rain' by The Move.

Jimi Hendrix in psychedelic gear copied from the eighteenth century.

Theatre

TREVOR NUNN WAS APPOINTED director of the Royal Shakespeare Theatre at the remarkably young age of 26. The play *Soldiers* by Ralph Hochhuth, which attacked Winston Churchill, was vetoed by the board of the National Theatre, though director Laurence Olivier and literary manager Kenneth Tynan were in favour of putting it on. In October the play opened to controversy in Berlin. Edward Albee, of *Who's Afraid of Virginia Woolf?* fame, scored a success with the play *A Delicate Balance*.

Sport

1967 WAS NOT NOTABLE for many major sporting achievements. Glasgow Celtic took the honours in becoming the first British football club to win the European Cup, Billy McNeil captaining the side to victory. In boxing Muhammad Ali showed supreme mastery. He beat Ernie Terrell in February so easily that one critic said 'The judges scored the fight by so wide a margin that had it not been for the world heavyweight championship it might well have been stopped'. Ali was practically unmarked, Terrell needed stitches.

On 2 September, American athlete Tommy Smith, holder of five world records, said that black American athletes should boycott the 1968 Olympic Games because of the 'lousy' racial situation in America.

A series of dramatic deaths

THE DANGERS OF SPACE EXPLORATION and pursuing speed records were emphasized in 1967 by a series of dramatic deaths. On 4 January Donald Campbell was killed in the speedboat *Bluebird* when going for the world waterspeed record. On 28 January, Gus Grissom and three other spacemen were burned to death in an Apollo spacecraft being tested on top of a Saturn rocket.

At 6.31:03 pilot Chaffee reported that a fire existed in the spacecraft. . . . At 6.31:09 senior pilot White repeated the previous report that there was a fire in the cockpit. At the same time the cabin pressure commenced to rise, and a large amount of motion was indicated by the inertial platform. This means that the crew were commencing their emergency egress procedure. At 6.31:12, or nine seconds after the first indication of fire, the cabin temperature started to increase rapidly and pilot Chaffee reported that a bad fire existed in the cabin. . . . No other intelligible communications were received, although some listeners believe there was one sharp cry of pain. Loss of radio signals occurred a few seconds later. . . .

Preliminary NASA report from Dr Robert C. Seamans, 3 February 1967

Grissom had been the first American to walk in space. On 31 January two more spacemen were killed in a fire in a space simulator in San Antonio, Texas. Then, on 25 April, Russian cosmonaut Komarov was killed after a space flight, when his parachute failed to open three to four seconds before landing.

The pursuit of speed claims a victim. Donald Campbell's Bluebird flips up in the air, then crashes backwards, killing Campbell.

Steps towards the moon

THE LESS SPECTACULAR but safer form of space exploration by unpiloted satellite probes continued. On 20 April the American Surveyor 3 made a soft landing on the moon. In June, Mariner 5 was sent to Venus by America while Russia sent the Venus 4 probe the same month. Two further Surveyor satellites landed on the moon, in September and November, and in October the Venus 4 probe dropped a package to the surface of Venus as it passed. On 31 October, Russia achieved the link-up of two unstaffed satellites which then uncoupled – a step towards building a space station. America progressed her moon programme in November when she tested a Saturn 5 rocket, which was capable of lifting the Apollo vehicle to the moon. On 14 December the USA and USSR agreed a pact to rescue astronauts in space.

Bombs and booms

ELSEWHERE, THE CHINESE exploded their first hydrogen bomb on 18 June, and on 4 November reports were printed that the Soviets were testing a space bomb – a fractional orbital bombardment system 100 miles up. Back nearer earth, on 18 June, anger over sonic booms by the supersonic Concorde led to so many people phoning the Ministry of Technology that the phones were jammed.

Medicine and physics: two milestones

TOWARD THE END OF THE YEAR, two major news items featured medicine and physics. On 5 December, Dr Christian Barnard performed the world's first heart transplant in South Africa. A living heart from a dead black person was put into the body of a white man, Louis Washansky. Although Washansky died soon after, it was a major development. Then, on 16 December, an artificial molecule was created at Standford University, California, by Dr Arthur Kronberg. Scientists claimed a fundamental secret of physics had been discovered.

1968 The year

Paris 1968: a student demonstrator emerges from a cloud of tear gas to throw a stone at police.

Youth in revolt

1967 HAD BEEN THE YEAR of the hippies and ideas of peace and love. 1968 was a year dominated by violence and the idea of revolutionary change. It was the year of the New Left – socialists who rejected both capitalism *and* communism – whose ideas inspired student revolts throughout the world.

The New Left argued that violence was caused by capitalism, and the continuing, escalating war in Vietnam, where the most powerful capitalist power was waging war on a small Asian country, gave weight to their ideas.

The student revolt

MANY STUDENTS WORLDWIDE were strong supporters of the Vietnamese against the United States. In February British students occupied Leicester University and there were demonstrations at Essex and Cambridge. Student demos followed in Poland (March), Japan (April), Columbia, New York (May), Frankfurt (May), Hornsey and Guildford (June). But the most spectacular student revolt took place in France.

Che Guevara, martyr of the Communist cause and inspiration figure behind the student revolution.

# of protest

Protest in Paris

ON 3 MAY, STUDENTS battled with police in the Latin Quarter of Paris. Courses were suspended in the Arts Faculty of the Sorbonne University, but more riots took place on 6 May, and the following day 10,000 students marched through Paris. Patrick Searle and Maureen McConville were the Paris correspondents for the *Observer* newspaper. They recalled the riots in their book, *French Revolution 1968:*

The night of the barricades, 10-11 May 1968, has passed into history. . . . Lit by the red glare from fires and under drifting acrid gas clouds, the battle raged for four hours, as the police – in charge after charge – drove the students from their defences, pinning them into an ever smaller redoubt [temporary shelter] from which they could escape only by braving the fury of rifle butts and truncheons. Residents of the [Latin] Quarter, horrified spectators of the savage mopping up operations, passed food and drink to the insurgents, doused them in water to allay the tear gas, and took fleeing and bleeding students into their houses, from which only too often they were snatched by the police. . .

Boys and girls threw themselves into the fighting with incredible abandon and dedication. To many young and high-keyed spirits, this was the chance to join the heroic revolution of Fanon*, Guevara and Debray*, to which they had so long thrilled. This was their Vietnam. . . . In this war game, the sinister and terrifying police – masked, helmeted, goggled, clad in gleaming black from head to toe – were cast in the role of evil spirits. . .

*Fanon and Debray were, like Guevara, leading figures in the revolutionary cause.

Rioting continued, with 367 people injured on 13 May. In protest against police violence, half a million people took to the Paris streets. Factory workers joined the students, using the atmosphere of protest to make their grievances felt. By 20 May, 120 factories were occupied and two million workers on strike for more pay and shorter hours.

De Gaulle's reaction

THIS WAS A CHALLENGE to the government of de Gaulle, as many thought the strike might lead to violent revolution. On 25 May the Paris Bourse (Stock Exchange) was set on fire after de Gaulle had appeared on television. On 30th May de Gaulle called up the French army to surround Paris and announced an election for June.

Frenchwomen, Frenchmen!
As the trustee of national and republican legitimacy, I have for 24 hours studied all possibilities. . . . I have taken my decisions.

In the present circumstances, I shall not resign. I have a mandate from the people. I shall fulfil it. . .

I am today dissolving the National Assembly. . .

As for the Parliamentary elections, they will take place within the period laid down by the Constitution, unless an attempt is made to gag the entire French people . . . by the same methods which are used to prevent the students from studying, the teachers from teaching, the workers from working. These methods are intimidation, deception, and tyranny.

President de Gaulle's speech to the nation, 30 May 1968

French election results, June 1968

	After	*Before*
Gaullists	294	197
Communists	34	73
PSU (Socialists)	–	3
Federation of Left	57	118
Independent Republic	64	43
Centre PDM	27	42
Others	9	9

With tanks in the Paris area and police evicting strikers from factories the situation looked grim. The employers eventually offered the unions more money for less work, however, and the strikes were called off. The police also succeeded in ousting students occupying the Sorbonne (Paris University), and the election at the end of June gave overwhelming support for de Gaulle – his party gained a majority of seats in the parliament. This was a decisive defeat for the Left, but it was remarkable that students could cause such a crisis that the government was forced to call an election.

The October demonstration

STUDENT PROTESTS and the Vietnam war came together in a series of demonstrations against the USA. The greatest of these, in Britain in October 1968, caused panic. Many, remembering events in May in France, feared the demonstrators would cause violence if not revolution.

On 5 September *The Times* carried a report that 'A small army of militant extremists plans to seize control of certain highly sensitive installations and buildings in central London during the demonstration'. It stated however, that 'Scotland Yard officially denied that they had received reports that "Molotov cocktails" [petrol bombs] have been made and that firearms might be used'. These fears were shown to be exaggerated when the demonstration took place with only minor incidents.

A Soviet tank in a Prague street.

Czechoslovakia

THE NEW LEFT's hopes of a different type of society which was neither Communist nor capitalist were boosted at the start of 1968 by developments in Czechoslovakia. In January, Dubcek replaced the old-style leader, Novotny, as head of the Czech Communists, and began to create a freer, more democratic society. In June, censorship was abolished. This alarmed Russia and the Warsaw Pact allies, and Dubcek and Brezhnev had talks in July. These did not satisfy Russia, and fearing Dubcek was abandoning communism, Russia invaded with four Warsaw Pact allies on 20 August. With 175,000 foreign troops in the country, Czechoslovakia had no chance of fighting back, and a pro-Soviet government was brought in. On 18 October the Czechs were forced to sign a treaty allowing Soviet troops to stay in their country.

China

ON 1 JANUARY, Mao Zedong, now 76, appeared at a rally to show he was still in control of the Cultural Revolution. Reports of riots still arrived – in January from Guangdong province in East China, in March from Guiyang and Shanxi province, in April from Shaanxi, Liaoning and Sichuan provinces. In May Liaoning province became the twenty-third province to set up a Triple Alliance Committee – leaving six to go – but the army had to protect the railway in Guangdong after anti-Maoist attacks. In August reports said that fighting in Guangdong was disrupting supplies to Vietnam. On 15 October, at the twelfth meeting of the Central Committee, Liu Shaoqui (Chairman of the People's Republic), was stripped of all his posts and expelled from the Party. He was described as 'The main traitor, workers' thief and Kuomintang [Nationalist Party] running dog'.

The USA

1968 WAS A TRAGIC YEAR in the USA. The justified bitterness of blacks in the country was underlined on 29 February when the President's National Commission on Civil Disorders said the main cause of riots was 'The racial behaviour of white Americans toward black Americans'. On 5 April, Martin Luther King was assassinated by white racist, James Earl Ray. Riots continued, with a serious uprising in Chicago in April leaving 11 dead.

More important for most Americans was the war in Vietnam. In April anti-war Democrat Senator McCarthy gained 42% of the votes in the Democratic primary election in New Hampshire, a clear vote against the Democratic President. Johnson, who announced he would not stand for re-election. Robert Kennedy then became the leading Democrat candidate, but the curse of the Kennedys fell on him on 6 May, when he was shot dead by a Lebanese immigrant, Sirhan Sirhan. Although a new President, Richard Nixon, was elected in November, it was clear that America's problems would continue.

The 'Tet Offensive'

AT THE END OF JANUARY the Vietcong showed how little real support the United States had in Vietnam when they launched attacks right in the middle of the capital city, Saigon, in the 'Tet Offensive'. On 31 January they attacked the American Embassy itself. The Americans beat them back, and the Vietcong lost 4959 men, but this attack and others in five other Vietnamese cities shocked the United States. The *New York Times* commented 'The contrast between the zeal of the enemy forces, and the slackness of the South Vietnamese is alarming'. On 29 February *Le Monde* outlined the problem presented to the Americans by the Tet Offensive:

The US government is faced with a choice as difficult as it is urgent – whether to continue to ensure the protection of the large towns and abandon a large part of the countryside to the National Liberation Front, or to strip the defences of the towns by sending US and government units into the countryside to resume a more offensive role. . . The effectives [soldiers] at General Westmoreland's disposal do not allow him to ensure the protection of both towns and the countryside while facing the threat of an offensive in the Northern Provinces.

Britain

THE LABOUR GOVERNMENT was still being criticized from both right and left. In January, the Prime Minister of Singapore, Lee Kwan Yew, attacked British plans for military withdrawal from east of Suez. George Brown, the Foreign Secretary, was also unhappy about this, and he resigned from the government in March. Plans for a continuing pay freeze angered Labour's union allies in the TUC, while the voters continued to swing to the Tories – an 18.4% swing in by-elections in March. In April, despite protests from within the Labour Party, the government announced 18 more months of prices and incomes restraint.

In September the TUC moved to the left and rejected the Prices and Incomes Policy. In a shock move, the Labour conference agreed, voting 5–1 against prices and incomes restraint. *The Times* commented, 'No Labour government has ever suffered such an overwhelming repudiation of fundamental policy as Mr Wilson and the cabinet suffered'. Harold Wilson still received a standing ovation from conference, however, and made it clear he did not intend to follow Labour Party Policy.

'Rivers of Blood'

RACISM BECAME A MAJOR issue in February when Tory Shadow Cabinet minister Enoch Powell made a speech predicting 'rivers of blood' if coloured immigration were not stopped. This caused an intense row, with dockers marching in favour of his views and students against. In April, Tory leader Ted Heath sacked Powell from the Shadow Cabinet. Nevertheless, as Asian people expelled from Kenya began to arrive in Britain in large numbers, the Labour government rushed through a bill limiting coloured immigration. Although the government also passed a Race Relations Bill, many people thought Labour had given in to racialism.

'The Troubles' in Northern Ireland

ANOTHER EXPLOSIVE ISSUE which became news in 1968 was Northern Ireland. Catholics, who felt they were being treated as badly as negroes in America, formed a civil rights group. On 4 October a civil rights march in Derry was banned after threats of a counter march by the Loyalist Orange Order. The march went ahead and 96 people were injured. The police were accused of 'entirely unprovoked violence' by Labour MPs, and Tim Jones, a reporter from *The Times*, claimed he was beaten up by half a dozen police while doing his job. This was the start of 'The Troubles' in Northern Ireland, with further riots in Derry in November.

The hippie dream collapses

THE BEATLES CONTINUED to hit the headlines. In February they visited India to study Transcendental Meditation with the Maharishi. But although the cartoon film based on Beatles music, *Yellow Submarine*, was a great success in July, other things did not go well. In January the Beatles set up Apple Corps Ltd, to promote 'Western Communism'. The hippie ideal of freedom proved a disaster. So much was stolen that in August the shop closed down and within six months the organization had lost £2 million.

The aims of Apple, according to John Lennon:

The aim isn't just a stack of gold teeth in the bank. It's more of a trick to see if we can get artistic freedom within a business structure – to see if we can create things and sell them without charging five times our cost.

According to Paul McCartney it was:

A controlled weirdness . . . a kind of Western Communism. We want to help people, but without doing it like a charity. . . . We're in the happy position of not needing any more money, so for the first time the bosses aren't in it for money. If you come to me and say, 'I've had such and such a dream', I'll say to you, 'Go away and do it'.

Business Report by Stephen Maltz, the Beatles' financial adviser:

As far as you were aware, you only had to sign a bill and pick up a phone and payment was made. You were never concerned where the money came from or how it was being spent and were living under the idea that you had millions at your disposal. . . . Your personal finances are in a mess. Apple is in a mess.

Quoted Philip Norman *Shout*, 1982.

In November, John Lennon was fined for possessing dope. The Beatles album of 1968, known as the 'White Album', was thought patchy. The Rolling Stones seemed to be more in tune with the times and their song 'Street Fighting Man' became the anthem of the students.

The Beatles, shown as cartoon characters for the film Yellow Submarine.

Films

IN MARCH, ZEFFERELLI's film *Romeo and Juliet* was released, starring 15-year-old Olivia Hussey. That spring saw *Planet of the Apes, Elvira Madigan*, Tony Richardson's *Charge of the Light Brigade*, Marlon Brando's *Reflections in a Golden Eye. Closely Observed Trains* was a memorable Czech film about a teenager falling in love in Nazi-occupied Czechoslovakia, and May saw Kubrick's *2001*. The hit film of the year was Mike Nichols' *The Graduate*, starring Anne Bancroft and Dustin Hoffman, about a student discovering sex and love.

Politics arrives in sport

IN SPORT, 1968 WAS A YEAR when even the greatest achievements were overshadowed by politics. Sporting headlines included the death of world champion racing driver Jim Clark, Manchester United's victory in the European Cup, and Virginia Wade's victory in the US Women's Open tennis championships. Then, in April, the International Olympic Committee removed South Africa from the Olympics because of apartheid. That August there was uproar when Basil d'Oliviera – a black exile from South Africa who played cricket in England – was dropped from the England Test side to play South Africa. Many argued this was done to satisfy the South African government. Then, in September, d'Oliviera was signed by a newspaper to report the Test series – and was banned by the South African government. When, a week later, Tom Cartwright dropped out of the Test side through injury, d'Oliviera was chosen to go in his place. The South Africans refused to accept the team with d'Oliviera and the tour was cancelled.

In October, the Olympics took place. Major sporting achievements, including a world record long jump of 29 ft 2½ in. by Bob Beamon – 1 ft 9¾ in. above the previous best – were overshadowed by Black Power protests. On 16 October Tommie Smith and John Carlos won gold and bronze in the 200 metres, and took their medals wearing black gloves and black scarves and giving a Black Panther salute (The Black Panthers were militant young blacks who tried to fight back against police violence.) Roger Bannister, the first four-minute miler, described this as 'A gesture conducted with dignity and poise and all very memorable', but when the winning trio in the 400 metres, Evans, James and Freeman made a similar gesture, Smith and Carlos were banned from the American team.

Science and Technology

In space

THE SPACE RACE CONTINUED in 1968 with both America and Russia making important steps forward. Russia continued her unstaffed programme of space exploration, sending Luna 14 to the moon in April and alarming the Americans in September by sending the Zond probe to the moon. It circled 1210 miles above the surface then returned safely to earth. This suggested the Russians were capable of sending a staffed mission to the moon and increased pressure on the American Apollo programme. In January the United States sent up an unstaffed capsule on the Saturn rocket, rehearsing for the moon mission. On 11 October Apollo 7 began a successful 11-day voyage round the earth. Then, from 21 to 27 December, Apollo 8 carried out a highly successful lunar trip, including ten orbits of the moon. This completely overshadowed the Russian achievement of sending a staffed spacecraft – Soyuz 3 – into earth orbit on 28 October. In November the Zond 6 spacecraft circled the moon, unstaffed, and returned. The space race was building to a climax.

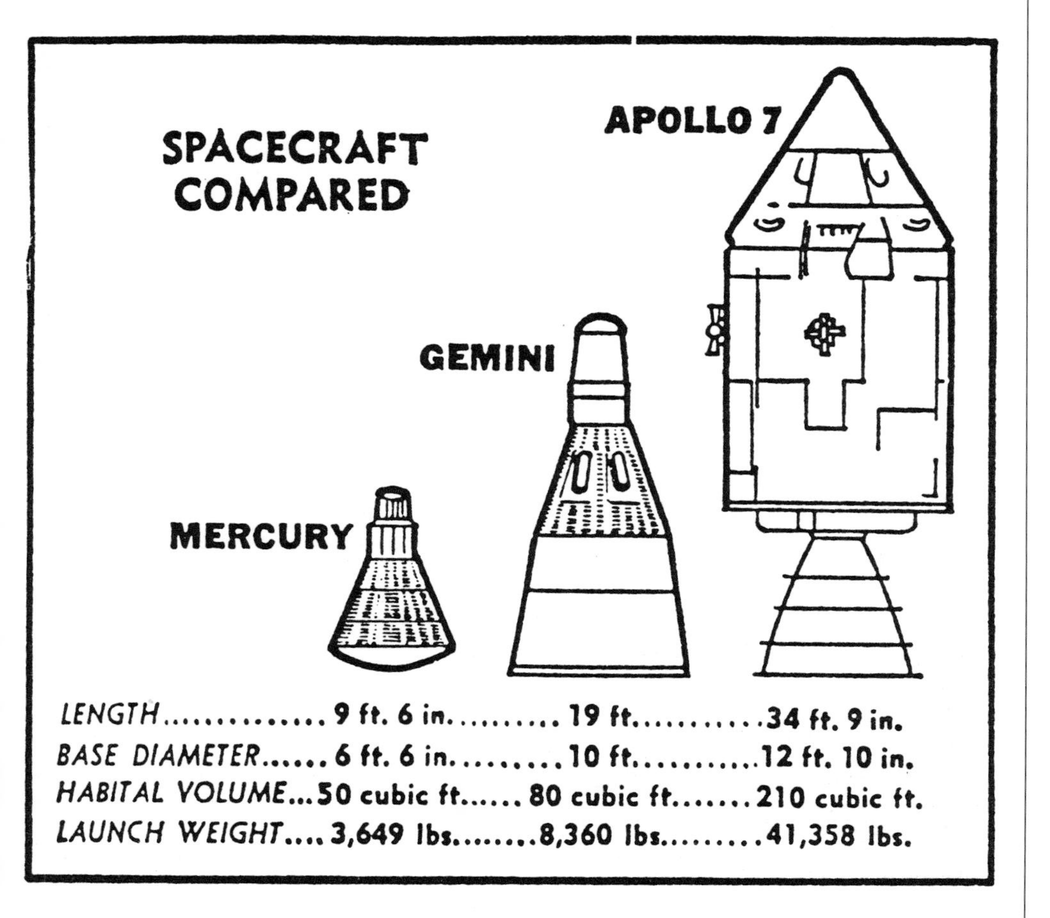

As America prepared for the moon shot, the satellites grew bigger. Mercury held one astronaut, Gemini two, Apollo three.

Down to earth

BACK ON EARTH the dangers of conventional travel were emphasized in March when Yuri Gagarin, the first man in space, was tragically killed in an air crash. There were further reminders that science was not foolproof. In May a block of flats at Ronan Point, in East London, was wrecked and three people killed when a gas cooker exploded. The same month an American nuclear submarine sank, and in October an American living in Britain got a six-year sentence for killing a girl while on an LSD trip. The latter story highlighted the dangers of widespread experimenting with 'mind expanding' drugs.

Scientific controversies

IN FEBRUARY THE FIRST British nuclear submarine tested a Polaris missile for the first time, adding to the controversy about nuclear weapons. Argument about science was not new. In July the Catholic Church said it was considering removing the charge of heresy against the scientist Galileo, who had argued in the sixteenth century that the earth went round the sun and had been persecuted by the Church as a result. The Church's attitude to science was questioned in the same month, however, by the Pope's rejection of birth control. In December 2,600 scientists at the American Association condemned the Pope's decision. Science took a step forward in November, however, when the US Supreme Court ruled illegal the notorious 'Monkey Law' of Arkansas. This had made it illegal to teach the scientific theory of evolution, which said that people were descended from monkeys.

1969 The Eagle

Apollo reaches upward

ON 21 JULY 1969 AN AGE-OLD DREAM reached fulfilment when people walked on the moon for the first time. The Apollo moon shot was not a single rocket which could travel to the moon and then come back in one piece, as writers such as Jules Verne (1828-1905) had predicted. In fact space travel was like a series of Chinese boxes. A huge Saturn 5 rocket blasted off, using up enormous amounts of fuel to escape earth's gravity and put the tiny spacecraft on course for the moon. The rocket itself then fell back to earth and burnt up. The spacecraft coasted at high speed to the moon and went into orbit around it. A small mooncraft (the Lunar Exploration Module – LEM) carrying two astronauts then dropped off and landed on the moon, leaving one astronaut circling the moon in the command module. After exploring the moon, the moonship (LEM) astronauts blasted off in the LEM and rejoined the command module. The command module then left the LEM behind and sailed back to earth, landing in the sea – a tiny piece of the huge package that had started off.

Most of the fuel was used up by the Saturn 5 rocket in the initial launch. The command module and LEM only had tiny amounts of fuel, and very little in reserve if anything went wrong. The astronauts had only a small supply of air, and if they took too long they would suffocate. Everything had to work first time.

has landed

Apollo 11 lifts off

THE THREE ASTRONAUTS were Neil Armstrong, Buzz Aldrin, and Michael Collins. At 0932, Florida time, on 17 July, Apollo 11 took off from Cape Kennedy space centre.

Apollo 11 is on its way to the moon. It carries three brave astronauts; it also carries the hopes and prayers of hundreds of millions of people here on earth, for whom that first footfall on the moon will be a moment of transcendent drama. Never before has man embarked on so epic an adventure.

In the words of the plaque the Apollo astronauts expect to leave on the moon, they go 'in peace for all mankind'. The adventure is not theirs alone, but everyone's; the history they are making is not only scientific history, but human history. That moment when man first sets foot on a body other than Earth will stand through the centuries as one supreme moment in human experience, and profound in its meaning for generations to come. . . .

President Nixon, 17 July 1969

After an uneventful flight, the astronauts went into moon orbit, and Armstrong and Aldrin transferred to the LEM for the flight to the moon's surface. At 2117 British time on 20 July, the LEM radioed back the historic message from the Sea of Tranquillity: 'Tranquillity base, the Eagle has landed'.

The famous picture of Edwin Aldrin walking on the moon, taken by astronaut commander Neil Armstrong.

The plaque left on the moon by the first astronauts, signed by the three voyagers and the American President, Nixon.

'One small step for a man. . .'

AFTER CAREFUL CHECKS that all the equipment was working, Neil Armstrong put on his spacesuit and stepped out of the LEM. As he went down the ladder on to the moon's surface he gave a running commentary:

'I'm at the foot of the ladder. The LM footpads are only depressed at the surface about one or two inches. Although the surface appears to be very finely grained as you get close to it, it's almost like a powder. . . . I'm going to step off the LM now. That's one small step for a man, one giant leap for mankind.

The surface is fine and powdery. I can pick it up loosely with my toe. It does adhere in fine layers like powdered charcoal to the sole and sides of my boots. I only go in a small fraction of an inch – maybe an eighth of an inch – but I can see the footprints of my boots and the treads in the fine sandy particles. There seems to be no difficulty in moving around, as we suspected. It's even perhaps easier than the simulations at one-sixth G [earth gravity] that we performed . . . on the ground. . . .

[The moon] has a stark beauty of its own. It's like much of the high desert of the United States. It's different, but it's very pretty out here.

HERE MEN FROM THE PLANET EARTH
FIRST SET FOOT UPON THE MOON
JULY 1969, A. D.
WE CAME IN PEACE FOR ALL MANKIND
NEIL A. ARMSTRONG ASTRONAUT
MICHAEL COLLINS ASTRONAUT
EDWIN E. ALDRIN, JR. ASTRONAUT
RICHARD NIXON PRESIDENT, UNITED STATES OF AMERICA

Armstrong then put up a plaque, signed by the three astronauts and President Nixon, bearing the message:

'Here men from the planet Earth first set foot upon the moon, July 1969 A.D. We came in peace for all mankind.'

At 0415 British time, Buzz Aldrin joined Armstrong on the surface and they planted the American flag. They spent the day exploring the surface and carrying out experiments, then blasted off to join the command module Columbia, still circling the moon.

Columbia was due back at 0550 British time on 24 July, splashing down in the Pacific 1000 miles south west of Honolulu. It arrived ten seconds behind schedule, within a mile of the target point – an amazing feat after travelling to the moon and back.

Worldwide recognition

THE AMERICAN SPACE ADMINISTRATION basked in worldwide praise. The Russians were allowed to see the return live on television and praised the 'courageous' Americans. The television channels estimated that 600 million people, one-fifth of the world's population, had watched the moon walk on television – the largest audience ever for a single event. America's space programme had scored its greatest triumph.

World News

Sino-Soviet relations improve

ON 5 FEBRUARY it was announced that the Chinese army was to be moved around the country to break links which some of its units had developed with groups supporting the Cultural Revolution. In March, border fighting with the Soviet Union began, and despite big anti-Russian demonstrations in Beijing, and comparisons of Mao with Hitler in Moscow, the real danger of major war between China and the USSR seems to have aided the more cautious figures in the Chinese Communist Party. In June the Communist Party decided to 'consolidate' (i.e. revive) the Young Communist League, the official Chinese Party youth organization, which had lost its popularity when Mao had formed the Red Guards. The Red Guard groups were now disbanded, and all bodies in China, including the army, were required to 'now carry out to the letter the line of the Party's Central Committee'. Despite border clashes with Soviet troops, or because of them, on 8 November the Chinese Party sent the Soviets an unusually friendly telegram. This spoke of the 'great friendship' of the Chinese and Russian. Many observers believe the Chinese Communist Party leaders were frightened of the danger of civil war inside China and war with Russia on the border, and decided to reverse the Cultural Revolution.

Protest continues

REBELLION STILL MADE THE HEADLINES. In January, students at the London School of Economics tore down security gates erected to prevent further sit-ins, and two lecturers, were disciplined for taking part. In April two lecturers Robin Blackburn and Nicholas Bateson, were sacked. In July student protest reached Eton, where a branch of the Schools Action Union was formed. The most dramatic events in the protest movement, however, concerned squatting – the taking over of empty buildings by homeless hippies. On 29 August, the London Street Commune took over a building at 144 Piccadilly which was due for demolition. Three hundred people set up home there, and when the police moved in to evict them the supposedly peaceful hippies showered them with missiles. The police cleared several other squats in September, which temporarily halted the squatting movement but not the problem of homeless people in London.

Social reform

STEPS WERE TAKEN to make divorce easier, and on 16 December MPs voted 343 to 185 in favour of making the abolition of hanging permanent.

US troops begin to withdraw from Vietnam

IN JANUARY, THE SCALE OF THE BATTLE facing the American-backed forces was revealed. One and a half million troops, including 550,000 American soldiers, and 800,000 South Vietnamese, faced 200,000 Vietcong guerrillas. Despite its overwhelming numerical superiority, the government was taking a beating. The total American war dead reached 33,630 in April, passing the total for the Korean war, and the Americans decided their losses were too high and began handing over to the South Vietnamese on 25 March. On 9 June, President Nixon announced he was withdrawing 25,000 men. It was clear the tide was turning in favour of the Vietcong, and though Ho Chi Minh, the Vietnamese Communist leader, died on 9 September, the writing was on the wall for the United States.

No matter what difficulties and hardships may lie ahead, our people are sure to win total victory. The US Imperialists will have to pull out. Our fatherland will be re-united. Our compatriots in the North and in the South will be reunited and under the same roof.

Our country will have the signal honour of being a small nation which, through a heroic struggle, has defeated two big imperialisms – the French and the American – and made a worthy contribution to the national liberation movement.

Extract from Ho Chi Minh's will, September 1969

Violence and protest in the USA

ON 20 JANUARY, RICHARD NIXON became President of the USA. He took over a country riddled with violence. On 11 March, James Earl Ray received a 99-year prison sentence for killing Martin Luther King. Liberal America was shocked when on 21 July Senator Edward Kennedy was involved in an accident in which a girl was killed. The car he was driving plunged into a river. He escaped, and there was speculation that he had not done enough to save her. Even more shocking, on 11 August film actress Sharon Tate and a group of friends were ritually murdered. Members of a hippie commune were charged with the murders on 2 December. The liberal dreams of the early 1960s seemed to be dying – but in October an estimated 36 million Americans took part in protests against the Vietnam War.

British troops sent to Northern Ireland

1969 WAS THE YEAR that Northern Ireland exploded into massive violence. In January a civil rights march from Belfast to Londonderry met with violence from militant Protestants. When police re-routed a subsequent civil rights march after receiving threats from the Protestant Ulster Volunteer Force, a riot broke out in Newry. Ian Paisley emerged as a major Protestant figure, whipping up Protestant feeling against civil rights for Catholics, and in April the British government sent troops to Ulster to reinforce the police against growing violence. When the Unionist premier, Terence O'Neill, tried to bring in One Person One Vote, the Unionist Party ousted him in favour of a hard-liner. Protestant Orange Order marches in July and August sparked off Catholic riots in Derry and Belfast, and on 14 August, British troops were sent into the Catholic ghettoes of Belfast and Derry to restore law and order. The following are three different views of 'The Battle of the Bogside'.

Eamon McCann, a civil rights worker:

This has nothing to do with civil rights. . . . It is a religious war, aggravated by the massive Catholic unemployment figures in Derry and by the bad housing conditions in the Bogside. [The Catholic area of Londonderry].

Cardinal Conway, Roman Catholic Archbishop of of Armagh and Primate of All Ireland:

I feel bound to say . . . that I cannot understand why a parade . . . was allowed to take place last Tuesday 12 August in a city which was tinder-dry. Neither can I understand why the police authorities found it necessary to ask their men to force their way into the Bogside area, where innocent people had been terrorised by some members of the police force on a number of previous occasions. It is quite obvious that the memory of those earlier nights of terror is still very much alive. . . .

Major Chichester-Clark, O'Neill's replacement as Unionist Prime Minister:

Well disciplined and ruthless men, working to an evident plan, attacked the police at a number of points in the city. The police were, of course, obliged to return their fire . . . the disorder which is being created in our capital city cannot and will not be tolerated. The police forces, dealing as they are with armed conspiracy, evidently require reinforcements.

British troops on the streets of Belfast.

Wilson presses for union reform

THE LABOUR PARTY CONTINUED to struggle to win support. In January the polls reported the Tories 20% ahead. Harold Wilson's plans for trade union reform ran into trouble within the Labour Party. In April, Wilson said the union bill was 'essential to the recovery of the nation', but the party executive committee voted against it. Then the TUC voted for a voluntary scheme for curbing unofficial strikes, and this was eventually accepted by the government. The balance of payments improved, and with an export boom the Tory lead was cut to 10% by December.

Films

1969 WAS A YEAR OF GOOD but not brilliant films. British films and film-makers were doing well; Richard Attenborough's *O What a Lovely War* and Karel Reisz's *Oliver!* (which carried off two Oscars) were unveiled in April. In June, Judy Garland died in London; the narcotics commission in New York revealed that she had been on drugs. When her doctors had suggested she take a year's rest, the film studio had rejected the suggestion, saying, 'We have $14 million tied up in her'. In August, a cinema-verité film about Bob Dylan, *Don't Look Back*, opened. Notable films of the autumn were the American *Midnight Cowboy*, British *Royal Hunt of the Sun*, and Continental *Z*.

Politics continues to dominate sport

POLITICS STILL DOMINATED SPORT. In June, Arthur Ashe, the black American tennis player, revealed that he had applied to play in the South African tennis championship and had been turned down. He argued South Africa should be boycotted by Davis Cup players, but the international tennis players, including two South Africans, voted 19-17 against the boycott. In England, the MCC unanimously invited the South African cricket team to tour in 1970. Opponents of apartheid set up to Stop the Seventy Tour, which organized demonstrations against the South African Rugby tour when it arrived in the autumn. Nevertheless, the Test and County Cricket Board still voted on 12 December for the tour to go ahead. Four days later, the South Africans confirmed they would only pick white players for their team. Pressure from various quarters eventually led to the MCC calling off the tour.

Pop and protest

IN POP MUSIC, the decline of the Beatles and the re-emergence of the Stones dominated the headlines. Paul McCartney married Linda Eastman on 12 March, and John Lennon married Yoko Ono on the 21st. George Harrison and wife Patti Boyd were arrested on dope charges on 14 March. These private affairs seemed more significant than Beatles music – when the album 'Abbey Road' appeared in December it got poor reviews. The Stones re-emerged to public view in the summer, giving a free concert to 250,000 people in London in June – just after the death of Brian Jones, one of the group's founder members – then undertaking a profitable American tour. The Stones tried to copy the successful hippy rock concert Woodstock with a free concert in California, which turned into a nightmare with four dead. The Stones issued 'Let It Bleed', the lyrics of which were mainly concerned with sex, drugs and violence, and John Lennon handed back his MBE as a political protest:

Of course, my action was a publicity gimmick for peace. I always squirmed when I saw MBE on my letters. I didn't really belong to that sort of world. I think the Establishment bought the Beatles with it. Now I am giving it back, thank you very much. Investitures are a waste of time. It's mostly hypocritical snobbery and part of the class system. I only took it to help the Beatles make the big time. I know I sold my soul when I received it, but now I have redeemed it in the cause of peace.

Melody Maker POP 30

1 (1) I HEARD IT THROUGH THE GRAPEVINE Marvin Gaye, Tamla Motown
2 (7) ISRAELITES .... Desmond Dekker, Pyramid
3 (2) GENTLE ON MY MIND .... Dean Martin, Reprise
4 (4) BOOM BANG-A-BANG .... Lulu, Columbia
5 (3) SORRY SUZANNE .... Hollies, Parlophone
6 (5) IN THE BAD OLD DAYS .... Foundations, Pye
7 (6) GAMES PEOPLE PLAY .... Joe South, Capitol
8 (16) GOODBYE .... Mary Hopkin, Apple
9 (12) WINDMILLS OF YOUR MIND .... Noel Harrison, Reprise
10 (17) PINBALL WIZARD .... Who, Track
11 (8) MONSIEUR DUPONT .... Sandie Shaw, Pye
12 (14) I CAN HEAR MUSIC .... Beach Boys, Capitol
13 (9) GET READY .... Temptations, Tamla Motown
14 (13) GOOD TIMES (BETTER TIMES) ...... Cliff Richard, Columbia
15 (15) FIRST OF MAY .... Bee Gees, Polydor
16 (10) WHERE DO YOU GO TO .... Peter Sarstedt, United Artists
17 (11) SURROUND YOURSELF WITH SORROW Cilla Black, Parlophone
18 (21) HARLEM SHUFFLE .... Bob and Earle, Island
19 (26) CUPID .... Johnny Nash, Major Minor
20 (18) IF I CAN DREAM .... Elvis Presley, RCA
21 (22) HELLO WORLD .... Tremeloes, CBS
22 (24) I DON'T KNOW WHY .... Stevie Wonder, Tamla Motown
23 (27) PASSING STRANGERS Sarah Vaughan and Billy Eckstine, Mercury
24 (19) WICHITA LINEMAN .... Glen Campbell, Ember
25 (25) ONE ROAD .... Love Affair, CBS
26 (20) YOU'VE LOST THAT LOVIN' FEELIN' Righteous Brothers, London
27 (29) ROAD-RUNNER ... Jnr Walker and the All Stars, Tamla Motown
28 (—) MICHAEL AND THE SLIPPER TREE .... Equals, President
29 (23) THE WAY IT USED TO BE ...... Engelbert Humperdinck, Decca
30 (—) COME BACK AND SHAKE ME .... Clodagh Rodgers, RCA

POP 30 PUBLISHERS

1 Jobete/Carlin, 2 Sparta, 3 Acuff-Rose; 4 Chappell, 5 Schroeder, 6 Schroeder/Welbeck; 7 Lowery/Chappell, 8 Northern Songs; 9 United Artists, 10 Fabulous; 11 Carlin; 12 Lieber Stoller, 13 Jobete/Carlin; 14 Francis Day and Hunter; 15 Abigail; 16 Mortimer, 17 Peter Maurice; 8 Keymore / Marc James; 19 Kags Music; 20 Carlin; 21 Bron; 22 Jobete/Carlin; 23 Francis Day and Hunter; 24 Carlin; 25 Dick James; 26 Screen Gems; 27 Jobete/Carlin; 28 GLH; 29 Maribus; 30 April.

u.s. top ten

As listed by "Billboard"

1 (1) AQUARIUS/LET THE SUNSHINE IN Fifth Dimension, Soul City
2 (2) YOU'VE MADE ME SO VERY HAPPY Blood, Sweat and Tears, Columbia
3 (7) IT'S YOUR THING Isley Brothers, T Neck
4 (6) ONLY THE STRONG SURVIVE Jerry Butler, Mercury
5 (3) DIZZY .... Tommy Roe, ABC
6 (4) GALVESTON .. Glen Campbell, Capitol
7 (8) HAIR .... Cowsills, MGM
8 (10) TWENTY-FIVE MILES Edwin Starr, Gordy
9 (5) TIME OF THE SEASON .. Zombies, Date
10 (11) ROCK ME ...... Steppenwolf, Dunhill

top twenty albums

1 (1) GOODBYE .. Cream, Polydor
2 (2) BEST OF THE SEEKERS Seekers, Columbia
3 (5) THE SOUND OF MUSIC Soundtrack, RCA
4 (3) DIANA ROSS AND THE SUPREMES JOIN THE TEMPTATIONS .. Diana Ross and Supremes and Temptations, Tamla Motown
5 (—) SCOTT 3 ...... Scott Walker, Philips
6 (8) HAIR ...... London Cast, Polydor
7 (10) OLIVER ...... Soundtrack, RCA
8 (4) ENGELBERT Engelbert Humperdinck, Decca
9 (6) ROCK MACHINE I LOVE YOU Various Artists, CBS
10 (13) 20/20 Beach Boys, Capitol
11 (15) GENTLE ON MY MIND Dean Martin, Reprise
12 (11) YOU CAN ALL JOIN IN Various Artists, Island
13 (9) POSTCARD .... Mary Hopkin, Apple
14 (18) THE WORLD OF VAL DOONICAN Val Doonican, Decca
15 (12) WORLD STAR FESTIVAL Various Artists, Philips
16 (18) FAMILY ENTERTAINMENT Family, Reprise
17 (—) LED ZEPPELIN .. Led Zeppelin, Atlantic
18 (—) ANDY WILLIAMS SOUND OF MUSIC Andy Williams, CBS
19 (14) THE BEATLES (Double Album) Beatles, Apple
20 (—) WORLD OF MANTOVANI Mantovani, Decca

By 1969 the charts included more black acts – 10 in the top 30 on 13 April, led by Tamla Motown and including reggae songs. The logo at the top was influenced by Flower Power graphics. (Below): New Rolling Stone Mick Taylor and Mick Jagger at the Stones' free concert in Hyde Park, Summer 1969.

Developments in air travel

ALTHOUGH THE APOLLO MOON SHOTS stole the headlines, many other important developments took place in 1969. In January, the Soviet supersonic airliner, the TU144, made its maiden flight, beating the Concorde into the air. Concorde took to the air on 2 March. More important than either in the history of air travel, however, was the maiden flight of the first jumbo jet, the Boeing 747, in February. On 4 June the 747 flew from Seattle to Le Bourget in France – a distance of 5160 miles – to show how the big new jets could transform long-distance air travel.

Space exploration

OTHER SPACE EXPLORATION apart from Apollo took place. In January the Soviets sent the Venus 5 probe to land on Venus, rapidly followed by Venus 6. The Soviets also put much effort into staffed space flight. In January they sent up two satellites – Soyuz 4 and Soyuz 5 – which docked. This was the first time staffed spacecraft had docked. British scientist Sir Bernard Lovell said 'This gives the USSR a four-year lead in assembling space equipment.' In July, the Soviets put up Soyuz 6 and 7 at the same time to perfect their techniques. Dr Eugene Shoemaker resigned from the US space agency, NASA, because it 'backed space spectaculars at the expense of science'. He opposed the Apollo missions because unstaffed probes could learn as much, more cheaply. The USA was now years behind Russia in assembling equipment in space.

America did, however, send a probe to Mars, the first of two Mariner probes being launched on 23 February. By the end of March, Mariner 7 was in trouble, but on 30 January Mariner 6 sent back brilliant pictures as it sailed past Mars. Mariner 7 passed two weeks later.

The Boeing 747 Jumbo jet could take 490 passengers and fly at 45,000 feet (15,000 metres) – a mile higher than other airliners.

America rediscovered

MEANWHILE, BACK ON EARTH, Thor Heyerdahl attempted to sail across the Atlantic from Morocco to the Caribbean in a reed boat, to show that America could have been discovered before Columbus. The party started out on 26 May, and on 22 July it arrived at Barbados, having travelled 1600 miles before having to be picked up by a passing yacht. The crew had been drawn from seven nations, and Heyerdahl considered that the way the multi-national crew had worked together was as important as the actual voyage. In a year of great exploration, it was a lesson as important as any of the scientific ones.

Time Chart

	World News	Sport and the Arts	Science and Technology
1960	(3 February) Macmillan's 'Wind of Change' speech. (22 March) Sharpeville massacre. (1 May) U2 spy plane shot down over USSR. (11 July) USSR agrees to buy Cuban sugar after US boycott. (15 September) General Mobutu takes over in Congo. (30 September) USA advises its citizens to leave Cuba. (6 October) Labour Party conference votes in favour of 'Ban the Bomb' motion. (November) John Kennedy wins the US Presidential election.	(April) Premiere of Pinter's play *The Caretaker*. (February) Premiere of Fellini's film *La Dolce Vita* in Italy. (May) Premiere of film *Saturday Night and Sunday Morning*. (June) Premiere of Robert Bolt's play *A Man for All Seasons*. (July) Premiere of John Osborne's play *The Entertainer*. (July) Premiere of Alan Resnais's film *Hiroshima Mon Amour*. (August) Alfred Hitchcock's *Psycho* arrives in Britain. (September) Rome Olympics: Herb Elliott takes gold in 1500 metres; Cassius Clay takes gold in Boxing.	(11 March) Pioneer V satellite launched for US for Venus. (15 May) Russians launch 4½ ton satellite – big enough for a man.
1961	(3 April) Aldermaston 'Ban the Bomb' march reaches London. (17 April) US backed 'Bay of Pigs' invasion of Cuba. (23 April) French Generals revolt in Algiers. (17 August) Berlin Wall goes up. (18 September) Committee of 100 'Ban the Bomb' demonstration in London. (4 October) Labour Party reverses its decision on the Bomb and backs Gaitskell. (30 October) Stalin's body removed from Red Square in Moscow.	(March) RSC announce Shaffer's *Royal Hunt of the Sun* to come. (March) Premiere of *One Way Pendulum* by N.F. Simpson. (June) Premiere of *Luther* by John Osborne announced. (June) Plan to raise Abu Simbel (Egypt) temple announced. (September) Premiere of *Big Soft Nelly* by N.F. Simpson. (September) Premier of Samuel Beckett's *Happy Days* in New York.	(12 April) USSR sends Gagarin up as first person in space. (5 May) USA sends Alan Shephard up as first American in space. (October) First operation involving stopping a heart.
1962	(19 March) Cease fire agreed in Algeria. (July) Algeria independent. (5 August) Nelson Mandela arrested for organizing strike in South Africa. (27 September) Conference of non-aligned nations calls for peace and disarmament. (October) Indo-China war breaks out. (20 October) US Navy ordered to stop missile-carrying ships headed for Cuba. (22 October) Kennedy orders 500 mile blockade around Cuba. (28 October) Kruschev agrees to remove missiles from Cuba if US agrees not to invade. (7 November) Nelson Mandela imprisoned.	(February) *Z Cars* series begins on British TV. (February) Oxford Union agrees to admit women. (March) Accrington Stanley resign from the Football League because of bankruptcy. (11 October) Vatican Council opens in Rome. (4 October) Beatles 'Love Me Do' is released. (September) Sonny Liston beats Floyd Patterson for World Heavyweight Title.	(20 February) John Glenn goes round earth three times in US Mercury space capsule. (July) Telstar launched. (December) USA and USSR agree to co-operate in space.
1963	(14 January) De Gaulle blocks British attempt to join EEC. (14 February) Harold Wilson elected leader of Labour Party. (April) Hot line set up between USA and USSR. (6 June) Profumo resigns, admitting he had lied to Parliament. (25 July) Limited H Bomb test treaty signed. (28 August) March on Washington led by Martin Luther King. (19 October) Alec Douglas Home becomes British Prime Minister. (22 November) Kennedy is assassinated.	(January) Alicia Markova, Britain's greatest Ballerina, retires. (January) Durenmatt's play *The Physicists* premiered. (January) Roman Polanski's film *Knife in the Water* arrives in Britain. (May) Hitchcock's film *The Birds* opens. (August) Film of *Tom Jones* with Albert Finney premiered. (November) Premiere of *The Servant*, with script by Harold Pinter. (December) Beatles climax year of triumph in Britain by appearing at the Royal Command performance.	(11 April) US Nuclear sub *Thresher* sinks. (June) Valentina Tereshkova first woman in space. (October) USSR announces it will not try to land man on moon.
1964	(11 May) Civil Rights bill passes through US Congress. (4 August) US claim ships attacked in Gulf of Tonkin. Congress allows President to attack North Vietnam. (October) Kruschev ousted. Breznhev becomes leader of USSR. (1 October) Chinese A bomb exploded. (15 October) Labour wins General Election in Britain. (November) Lyndon Johnson wins US Presidential election.	(January) Royal Shakespeare Theatre announces 'Theatre of Cruelty'. (26 February) Cassius Clay beats Sonny Liston to take World Heavyweight boxing title. (28 March) Radio Caroline, first pirate radio station, on the air. (April) Beatles have top 5 in US charts.	(3 February) Ranger 6 becomes first US probe to reach the moon. (20 March) Louis Leakey discovers Homo Habilis remains. (9 April) US launches first Gemini mission. (July 17) Donald Campbell sets world land speed record at 403 mph. (28 July) Ranger 7 lands on moon, takes pictures. (16 October) China explodes its first atom bomb.

Time Chart

1965

World News

(8 March) Selma police attack Civil Rights demonstration : 67 injured.
(26 May) US Congress passes bill guaranteeing black voting rights.
(19 April) 15,000 strong anti-Vietnam War demonstration in Washington.
(13 August) Start of Watts Riots, Los Angeles.
(11 November) Southern Rhodesian UDI.

Sport and the Arts

(6 January) George Devine quits as director London Royal Court Theatre.
(19 January) *My Fair Lady* opens in London.
(1 April) Antonioni's *The Red Desert* (*Il Deserto Rosso*) opens.
(3 June) Dick Lester's film *The Knack* wins Grand Prix at Cannes.
(16 June) Eric Heffer MP congratulates Queen for giving Beatles MBE.
(1 July) *A Patriot for Me* by John Osborne opens.

Science and Technology

(18 March) Russian Cosmonaut Leonov first person to walk in space.
(6 April) Early Bird becomes first commercial space satellite.
(6 August) Russian Luna probe photographs far side of the moon.
(9 October) Harold Wilson opens Post Office Tower in London.
(25 October) Gemini 6 completes first docking in space.

1966

World News

(9 March) De Gaulle announces that France will leave NATO.
(31 March) Labour wins General Election in Britain with 98 seat majority.
(30 April) Zhou Enlai announces start of Cultural Revolution in China.
(6 June) James Meredith shot on Civil Rights march.
(14 November) Two million Red Guards demonstrate in Beijing.
(20 December) Male homosexuality legalized in Britain.

Sport and the Arts

(11 February) Paperback version of *The Lord of the Rings* announced.
(20 July) England wins the World Cup at soccer.
(August) Bob Dylan is involved in a motorcycle accident and withdraws from public view. His *Blonde on Blonde* double album becomes a landmark of the new psychedelic pop music.
(29 August) Beatles play their last live concert in California.

Science and Technology

(7 January) US Air Force loses H Bomb off Spain.
(4 February) Luna 9 makes first soft landing on moon.
(7 April) US Air Force finds its lost H bomb.
(16 September) Gemini 11 record height for staffed flight at 853 miles.
(27 October) Early Bird 2 satellite placed in orbit.
(8 December) USA and USSR sign treaty banning weapons in space.

1967

World News

(5 June) Israel attacks Egypt and Jordan at start of Six Day War.
(21 June) Muhammad Ali given five year sentence for refusing draft. Ali appeals.
(13 July) President Johnson drafts 100,000 extra troops for Vietnam, bringing total US forces to 500,000.
(19 July) Labour Government in Britain decides to withdraw forces from East of Suez.
(26 October) Mao Zedong dismisses ultra left from Central Committee of Chinese Communist Party.
(16 November) Labour Government devalues pound.

Sport and the Arts

(10 January) *The Sound of Music* becomes most popular film in British film history with 23 million viewers, overtaking *Gone With the Wind*.
(31 March) Miles Kington starts the *Times*' first pop column.
(1 June) Beatles *Sergeant Pepper* released.
(8 June) Clint Eastwood's *A Fistful of Dollars* released.
(24 June) Beatles sign an advert calling for legalization of cannabis.
(September) British BBC pop channel Radio One starts.
(7 September) Cult film *Bonnie and Clyde* opens in Britain.

Science and Technology

(20 April) Surveyor 4 US Moon probe makes soft landing.
(18 June) Chinese explode their first H bomb.
(31 October) Two unstaffed USSR space vehicles dock and undock – an important step towards building space stations.
(5 December) World's first heart transplant.
(14 December) USA and USSR sign pact to rescue space explorers if in trouble.
(16 December) Artificial molecule created at Stanford University.

1968

World News

(5 January) Dubcek replaces Novotny as Czechoslovak President.
(31 January)Tet Offensive begins in Vietnam.
(5 April) Martin Luther King killed.
(6 May) Robert Kennedy killed.
(13 May) 500,000 demonstrate in Paris against police violence.
(30 June) Second stage of French election, called in response to crisis, gives De Gaulle emphatic victory.
(20 August) Warsaw pact forces invade Czechoslovakia to stop Dubcek's reforms.

Sport and the Arts

(21 April) South Africa dropped from Olympics by International Olympic Committee.
(17 July) Beatles *Yellow Submarine* cartoon film opens in London.
(30 July) Beatles Apple boutique closes.
(16 October) US athletes Smith and Carlos stage black power demonstration at the Olympic games.
(18 October) Bob Beamon establishes world long jump record of 29 feet 2½ inches.

Science and Technology

(28 March) Yuri Gagarin killed in air crash.
(8 April) Luna 14 probe successfully sent to Moon by Russians.
(11 October) Apollo 7 11-day voyage round the earth.
(28 October) Russian staffed satellite Soyuz 3 in earth orbit.
(December) Apollo 8 successful voyage round moon – 10 orbits.

1969

World News

(5 February) Chinese Army to be moved around country to break up Red Guard groups.
(2 March) Border clashes begin between USSR and China.
(2 April) Total of US dead in Vietnam at 33,630 passes total in Korean War.
(9 June) US withdraws 25,000 troops from Vietnam.
(21 July) Edward Kennedy involved in Chappaquidick death.
(14 July) Riots in Derry start season of riots in Northern Ireland.
(11 August) Sharon Tate murdered.
(14 August) British troops sent to Derry and Belfast in response to riots.
(2 December) Charles Manson charged with Tate murders.
(9 December) Ho Chi Minh dead.

Sport and the Arts

(12 March) Paul McCartney marries Linda Eastman.
(26 March) John Lennon marries Yoko Ono.
(7 June) Stones play free concert in Hyde Park, London.
(August) Woodstock Festival – Peace, Love and Music – in USA.
(20 November) John Lennon sends back his MBE.
(7 December) Stones free concert, Altamont, California: four dead.
(12 December) Test and County Cricket Board vote for Cricket test tour by South Africans.
(16 December) South Africans confirm they will only pick whites.

Science and Technology

(1 January) Russian supersonic passenger jet TU144 maiden flight.
(5 January) Russian Venus 5 probe launched to soft-land on Venus.
(14 January) Russian Soyuz 4 and 5 launched to perform first docking by staffed space vehicles.
(30 January) US Mariner 6 takes pictures of Mars.
(10 February) 747 Jumbo Jet makes first flight.
(2 March) Concorde's first flight.
(26 May) *Ra I* starts voyage.
(4 June) Boeing 747 sets distance record with flight from Seattle to Paris.
(22 June) *Ra I* party arrives in Barbados.
(17 July) Apollo 11 lifts off for the moon.
(20 July) Apollo 11 Lunar Exploration Module lands on the moon.
(24 July) Apollo 11 returns to earth after successful moon shot.

Key figures of the decade

Muhammad Ali (1942-)

World Heavyweight Champion boxer, known as Cassius Clay till converting to the Black Muslim faith. Became Olympic Light-Heavyweight Gold Medal winner in 1960. World Heavyweight champion after beating Sonny Liston in 1964. Articulate and charismatic supporter of black rights, was stripped of title for refusing to fight in Vietnam. Regained title 1974.

Neil Armstrong (1930-)

Astronaut, graduate Purdue University, flew 78 combat missions in Korean War; shot down once. As civilian test pilot, flew X15 rocket plane capable of 4000 mph. As commander Gemini 8 on 16 March 1966, completed first docking with unmanned space vehicle. Chosen to command moon mission. 21 July 1969, became first person to walk on moon.

Joan Baez (1941-)

US Folk influenced pop singer. Came to fame at Newport folk festival 1959. First recorded 1960, Fourth Album popularized 'We Shall Overcome'. Tenth album set of Dylan songs. Had well publicized affair with Dylan, known as 'King and Queen of folk'. 1965, founded Institute for study of non-violence. In seventies moved toward rock music.

Beatles (1960-1971)

George Harrison (1943-), Paul McCartney (1942-), John Lennon (1940-1980), Ringo Starr (1940-). Formed in 1960 out of a Liverpool skiffle Group, turned to rock and roll, made first record 1962, first British No 1. 1963. All top five US singles April 1964. Consistently successful till break-up in 1971. The most important and influential pop group of the decade.

Leonid Brezhnev (1906-1982)

Russian Leader. Trained as an engineer, he worked his way up through the Communist Party. Assisted Kruschev in the 1950s but joined the opposition to him in the early sixties and replaced Kruschev as First Secretary, and thus Leader of the Communist Party, in 1964. Supported North Vietnam against the USA and continued opposition to Mao, but avoided war with US or China.

Fidel Castro (1926-)

Cuban leader. Led revolt against pro-American regime, won three-year guerrilla war, became ruler of Cuba January 1959. Became increasingly pro-Communist and Allied with USSR against USA. Import of Russia missiles led to Cuban missile crisis, 1962.

Charles De Gaulle (1890-1970)

French President. Led 'Free French' forces in World War Two, elected President 1958 because of Algerian crisis. Negotiated independence of Algeria from France in 1962; attacked by OAS generals for doing so. In 1968 defeated Student and Communist unrest by threats of force backed by election victory.

Alexander Dubcek (1921-)

Slovak Communist leader. Became head of the Slovak Party in 1963, and then of the whole Czechoslovak Party in 1968. He tried to introduce 'Socialism with a human face' but was stopped by Russian invasion. Lost office 1969, sent to Turkey as ambassador and was then completely disgraced.

Bob Dylan (1941-)

US Pop superstar. Emerged as a folk singer in New York 1960-61. Made name as protest singer 1961-64. Turned to rock and roll in 1965, then had serious motor bike accident in 1966 which stopped him from performing until 1968. Returned as hero to student generation interested in mysticism and drug related experiences.

Key figures of the decade

Yuri Gagarin (1934-1968)

Cosmonaut. Born Gzhatsk, USSR, son of a carpenter. Joined Soviet air force 1957. Launced in Vostok I from Tyuratom in Kazakstan, on 12 April 1961. First human in space. Made single orbit 327 km high, at 28,096 km per hour. After 108 minutes in space returned safely by parachute. Killed in air accident.

Hugh Gaitskell (1906-1963)

Leader of the Labour Party. A government minister in Attlee's Government, he was elected Leader of the Party in 1955. After the loss of the 1959 election, he campaigned to change Labour's socialist image, and when the Party adopted a ban-the-bomb policy in 1960, worked to reverse this in 1961. Died suddenly in 1963.

Che Guevara (1928-67)

Argentinian revolutionary. Fought with Castro's guerillas and became a high ranking minister, but left Cuba to carry out revolutionary Maoist activities in Latin America. Began guerilla warfare in Bolivia; killed by Bolivian army. Became a hero, particularly to student leftists.

Ho Chi Minh (1890-1969)

Vietnamese Communist leader. When young worked in France. Became a Communist, founded Indochinese Communist Party in 1930. Led anti-Japanese guerillas in World War Two; drove out French after bitter war 1945-54. Leader of North Vietnam until his death; fought the US backed South Vietnamese and laid the basis for victory.

Mick Jagger (1943-)

Lead singer of Rolling Stones. Joined Stones in 1960 when at London School of Economics. 1963 sang on first Stones record. In 1965 co-wrote Stones first US Number One, 'Satisfaction'. 1967 arrested on drugs charges. In 1968-69 appeared to sanction violence: Altamont concert in 1969 left four dead.

Lyndon Baines Johnson (1908-73)

US President. Vice-President 1960-63, became President on death of Kennedy. Re-elected in 1964. Successful on domestic front, especially on Civil Rights, he committed US forces to fight in Vietnam. The subsequent disasters forced him to quit as President in 1968.

John Fitzgerald Kennedy (1917-63)

US President. Son of a millionaire, was a war hero, entered politics and was elected the youngest ever President of the USA in 1960. Promised a vigorous 'New Frontier' policy at home, but was blocked by conservative interests. Abroad, had to deal with Berlin Wall and Cuban Missile crises. His murder shocked the world.

Martin Luther King (1926-68)

US black leader. Became leader of civil rights movement after Montgomery bus boycott of 1956. Led march on Washington 1963. Campaign of non-violence less influential as black militancy increased in mid sixties. Murdered by racist in 1968.

Nikita Sergeyevich Kruschev (1894-1971)

Russian Leader. Took over shortly after the death of Stalin in 1953. Moved toward 'peaceful co-existence' with the West, rejecting the idea that war was inevitable. The Chinese disagreed, leading to the Sino-Soviet split. Kruschev was removed from power in 1964.

Harold Macmillan (1894-1986)

British Prime Minister. Conservative politician, benefitted from prosperity of the 1950s. A very skilful politician, nicknamed 'Supermac'. Won the 1959 election on the slogan 'You've never had it so good'. Less successful after 1959, especially over Profumo. Resigned 1963 due to bad health.

Mao Zedong (1893-1976)

Chinese Communist Leader. Led Chinese Communists to victory after Civil war in 1949. Lost some power after failure of economy in 1959 and Sino-Soviet split 1960, but came back to supreme power during the Cultural Revolution (1966-69), which he master-minded.

Richard Millhouse Nixon (1917-)

US President. Vice President under Eisenhower, narrowly beaten by Kenney in 1960. Won the Presidency in 1968 and though conservative began to withdraw from Vietnam. Hated by students, was re-elected in 1972 but forced to resign over Watergate affair.

Harold Wilson (1916-)

Labour Leader, Prime Minister. Linked with the left-wing opposition to Gaitskell, but was elected Leader in 1963. Won the elections of 1964 and 1966, but did not fully solve Britain's economic problems. Policies of austerity annoyed the socialists while voters went Tory.

Books for further reading

David Arnold, *Britain, Europe and the Modern World 1871-1971*, Edward Arnold, 1973

Asa Briggs, *A Social History of England*, Weidenfeldt, 1983

Elizabeth Campling, *Living Through History: The 1960s*, Batsford, 1988

R.J. Cootes, *Britain since 1700*, Longman, 1968

Peter Cowie (ed.) *A Concise History of the Cinema, Vol. 2*, Zwemmer, 1971

T.K. Derry and T.L. Jarman, *The European World 1870-1975*, Bell and Hyman, 1977

M.N. Duffy *In Your Lifetime*, Basil Blackwell, 1969

Josh Dunson, *Freedom in the Air*, International Publishers, 1965

Emmett Grogan, *Ringolevio*, Panther, 1974

Felix Green, *Vietnam! Vietnam!*, Penguin, 1967

George Melly, *Revolt into Style*, Penguin, 1972

Phillip Norman, *Shout!*, Corgi, 1982

Purnell's History of the Twentieth Centurys, Vols 9, 10 and 11

Patrick Seale and Maureen McConville, *French Revolution 1968*, Penguin, 1968

John and Gwenneth Stokes, *Europe and the World, 1870-1970*, Longman, 1973

L.E. Snellgrove, *The Modern World Since 1870*, Longman, 1968

The Times January 1960 December 1969

Acknowledgments

The Author and Publishers would like to thank the following for permission to reproduce illustrations: The Camera Press Ltd for pages 3, 8, 10, 14, 20, 22, 25, 27, 30, 31, 33, 34, 35, 38, 39, 40, 41, 42, 43, 44, 52, 54; CBS records for page 16; The *Daily Mirror* for page 24; The Keystone Press Agency for pages 9, 17, 18, 23, 26, 47, 53, 65; The *Melody Maker* for page 64; NASA for page 60; The Photo Source Ltd for pages 5, 6, 11, 28, 29, 36, 46, 48, 56, 63; Shelter Picture Library for page 45 and Times Newspapers Ltd for page 49.

Index